"I read *Darkness Overturned* in one afternoon. Wow. What a compelling story –and so beautifully written. Patricia has a gift, and her use of metaphors and similes is wonderful." –Suzi A.

"It is the most incredible book I have ever read. I want to tell everyone, I really want to shout from the top of my lungs about how amazing this book is. It's the story, the words, the spirit, the hope…everything!" –Melissa M.

"Jane Goodall, in her book *Reason for Hope*, talks about the indomitable human spirit. If ever there was one, it is Patricia Struntz. For someone to have gone through what Patricia has gone through, and to emerge with such grace and beauty and love, is truly humbling." –Céline H.

"I got the book mid-day and spent the afternoon reading it. Actually, I cried, laughed, sighed, screamed, prayed and praised my way through it. I couldn't put it down." –Veronica M.

"Quakers say you must always speak truth to power and you will prevail. EsthersChild not only survived, she prevailed." –Pam J.

"This book may be more or less aimed at female readers, but it meant much to me as a male reader. I can hardly find words to say exactly how this book made me feel. I know that from the bottom of my heart I would like to apologize on behalf of the male species for the treatment EsthersChild received at the hands of other males. I found myself yelling at Saintman as I read. Talk about involved! –Farrell H.

"I am an avid reader, devouring five to ten books a week, but this last week I read only one, *Light Through the Dark Glass*. This book came along at a good time...just when the shadows were falling once again. I was reminded by EsthersChild that there is hope for entire healing, for complete victory."   –Anonymous

"I liked the abstract names in the book, like Saintman, Girl-Child, and BrightEyes. At first I thought I would not be able to connect to theses names, but in the end I realized that it made it easier. It made me feel all the time that this is not an invented story, but a story about real people that the author did not want to mention directly."   –Simone K.

"As old as I am (74), I have never read of such a living example of overcoming so much adversity by an indomitable will. *Darkness Overturned* is an inspiration for all who are fortunate enough to read it."   –Laura M.

"I finally let myself read EsthersChild's book...Like many other things, I guess I was afraid it might bring me back to life...(but now) I don't feel so alone anymore."   –Anonymous

Darkness Overturned

Darkness Overturned

EsthersChild

Darkness Overturned

Published by Wheatmark™
610 East Delano Street, Suite 104
Tucson, Arizona 85705 U.S.A.
www.wheatmark.com

International Standard Book Number: 978-1-58736-825-7
Library of Congress Control Number: 2007924400

rev201501

Contents

Preface

Running. So much of my life I've spent running. Not always away from, but often *to*—only to discover, in Alice-in-Wonderland fashion, a mirrored distortion of life, where direction seems reversed, absurd, and horrifying. Spiraling up, maybe down, I lost my bearings and cried again and again to the God who is neither up nor down, but everywhere.

I'm sure He often drew close enough to me that His breath warmed my shivering soul. Perhaps He even caught me up in His great arms of love, but I could not tell. Thus, as I cried out to God, so called He unto me, until He could at last be heard by me. And then I found Him, "Abba, my Father."

Every day was my heartache bitter. I was exhausted with groaning. I thought, If only I knew how to find God! I'd run to Him—tell Him everything: how unfair, how confusing this world is to me. My mouth would be full of arguments: I didn't choose this! And when He answered me, I would understand, at last.

Would He condemn me because of my weakness and ignorance? No! He would put strength in me, because He knew my dispute was not really with Him, but with the wrong that I could not comprehend.

Yet my experience was this: Behold, I ran forward toward God, but He was not there. (Was it forward?) Then I turned and ran backward, but still could not perceive Him. With panic, I looked to my left (where I knew He worked), but could not see Him. It seemed as though He even hid Himself on my right, so that I could not catch a glimpse of Him.

But, in fact, He always knew exactly which way I was going—how bewildered I was, how foolish—and when He was finally able to penetrate my darkened mind, He brought me forth as gold tried in the fire.

—Paraphrased from Job 23:1-10

Why EsthersChild?

There are several reasons why I chose for myself the name "EsthersChild." The Esther of biblical antiquity "had neither father nor mother"—and in a real sense, neither have I (Esther 2:7, NIV).

Esther's story is not unclouded. Though she is now accepted as a shining example of courage and faithfulness, her passage to greatness led through a harem of concubines.

Perhaps the one text in Scripture that captures best the cry of my heart through the agony of my quest for God was spoken by Esther: "I will go to the king, even though it is against the law. And if I perish, I perish (Esther 4:17, NIV).

No matter how "fallen" a child of humanity I was, I had but one goal—to go before the King. There were times when I felt that I had entered His throne room outside of the context of acceptable Christian standards, but I was always compelled to do so by my great need for Him. And always, He was pleased with me and held out to me the scepter of His healing power. By this I know forevermore that it is indeed "[my] Father's good pleasure to give [me] the kingdom" (Luke 12:32).

Chapter One

In the Beginning, Hurt

A scream pierced my mind, and I bolted up in bed, fully awake. I heard it again: long and high and sobbing. It was my mother's voice! A whimper formed on my lips, only to rush backward into my throat.

I jumped out of bed, threw open the bedroom door, and ran into the moonlit hall. Though only six years old, I was already familiar with the stench of alcohol that hung in the air. A dull thumping sound seemed to come up from the floor below. I moved to the top of the stairway, and in the dim light I saw my father at the foot of the stairs, straddling my mother at her waist, his hands locked over her throat. The long hairs that were usually combed neatly over the top of his balding head swayed rhythmically in front of his face as he brought my mother's head down to the floor again and again.

My father was a tall, large man—not muscular, but fat. Though he was a successful real estate salesman, he mostly wore blue-striped bib overalls, filled to capacity.

My mother wasn't screaming anymore. Slight of frame, she was no match for him. For a moment I was mesmerized by the scene. Then I saw my father's hunting knife, unsheathed, only inches away from his hand. I knew instantly that he intended to use it on her.

Into my mind flashed the image of a bearskin rug on the floor of my parents' bedroom, its terrible mouth frozen open in a silent roar. My father often bragged how he had killed it. He liked killing. Another of his trophies, an antlered deer head, hung on a living-room wall, its doleful eyes lifeless and staring. My body shook violently as I recalled the bloody carcasses that hung on meat hooks at the packing company where my father took his kills.

Again I heard a scream, but this time it was my own, echoing off the walls and down the stairwell. It must have pierced my father's drunken brain, because he stopped his attack on my mother and looked up at me. To this day, that is the picture that I remember of my father. And I cannot stand the smell of raw meat and alcohol.

I don't remember much after that: only that my mother slept on the foot of my bed that night. For years I could go to sleep at night only when I was sure that my parents were asleep. And I kept having a nightmare that my father had murdered my mother. I could hear her calling for me and finally found the top half of her, life-size but flat like a piece of plywood, lying on the floor of the inside balcony that overlooked the stairway. She had no arms and never comforted me. I always comforted her. And that part, at least, turned out to be painfully true to life. In my tormented dreams as a little girl, I perceived a reality that held true clear up to my mother's passing.

My relationship with my mother was always two-dimensional—and barely that. I grew up believing that I was never meant to be. Unplanned, I was conceived before my parents married. Since I followed the birth of an equally illegitimate brother by only fourteen months, I was scarcely a welcome newcomer to the family. To make matters worse, my brother was born lame in one leg. My birth interrupted only slightly my mother's obsession with caring for him. When I was older she propped me up with pillows and a bottle, and then cradled him. I grew into childhood accepting this favoritism. It was all I had ever known.

I loved my mother fiercely, but she took little notice of me. No time was exclusively mine. Any attention diverted my way was stolen from my brother. One night she came to my bed to comfort me. Though I no longer remember why, I was crying hard. As she took me in her arms she whispered, "I'm not doing this because I love you. I'm doing this so you'll shut up. You're keeping your brother awake."

I came to feel that nothing really belonged to me. I was never to touch my brother's toys, never to enter his room—but my things were to be shared. When we fought, which was often, he beat me over the head with my own teddy bear. His was off limits. If he won, I was told to be quiet. If I ever got the best of him, I was punished. And so a cavity of spirit began to form deep within my heart. Coupled with the horrible fear I had of my father, it was as if the little boat of my budding person-hood was set adrift on a large, uncharted sea, a crumpled and threadbare teddy my only companion. And I didn't want the teddy.

What becomes of little girls and boys whose lives are so conceived and thwarted? How many derelicts could trace, if they were able, their destitution and despondency to those tender, early years of character formation? How many marriages go awry because of leftover, unresolved debits carried into adulthood like hobo packs on a stick from childhood? And when, over a sawdust floor, such "sinners" are called to repentance, does Calvary automatically equalize all the hurt and damage sustained while living in this hostile world?

It is too easy to assume that a happy life naturally follows becoming a Christian, that failure only dogs the steps of the half-converted. Admonished to seek the will of God, believers are prone to measure sincerity in themselves and others by how well they are living their lives. With the abundance of scriptural promises of divine guidance, how could someone who is truly being led by God ever fall?

This book is not for theologians. It is for believers who have found that their sense of self-worth has all but been destroyed by repeated failure. It is for those whose potential for personal achievement seems forever thwarted. It is for those who weep in the shadows but hide in the sunshine, lest other believers find them in disrepute.

I am one of you.

I was born into emotional Babylon—confusion— where my identity was left for me to retrieve like an unmarked package.

When just one month short of seventeen, I accepted Christ as my Savior. I was so excited! Everything was going to be all right. The awful jumble of unhappiness that had been mine since birth would now give way to the well being surrounding those who are the children of God. No one explained to me that I might still be terribly torn by the circumstances of this life, that within *me* were tangled threads that even the Master Craftsman could not easily unwind and weave into a bright and lovely tapestry.

Who could have guessed that trouble would follow after me like an unpaid landlord, abusive and punishing? I loved God so much—what I knew of Him! My innocence seemed to underscore the absoluteness of my safety.

Fortunately, life is not static, and so these pages are also the story of my victory. Not the immediate victory of a well-trained army, but of relentless determination: I wanted God and He wanted me. Though I might have given up, He never did. With every heartache, He gave me more of Himself. With every humiliation, He offered the hope of excellence. Discouragement He met with compassion; bewilderment, with promise. It would take time, but miracles often do.

Chapter Two

The Closet Window

Board by board you build a house, brick by brick a wall. Thought by thought you make a man, inch by inch he's tall. And so we are the sum of the events of our lives, whether we remember them or not.

I remember very little of my early life. The year I was nine, my family traveled to Europe. I kept a diary that half year we were there, but it has always bothered me to read it. It's like reading someone else's journal. How could I have been to all those places and not remember?

What I do remember is Switzerland, my father's homeland. It suited me beyond my imagining, to my mother's dismay. She so hated my father that she wanted my brother and me to hate all that had to do with him with the same intensity that she did. My father I feared, but Switzerland I loved passionately!—the high meadows, the quaint architecture, the wondrously joyous music, and the smell of freshly carved wood. Cuckoo clocks, little wooden dancing bears, Swiss chocolate and cheese, the sound of distant cowbells—it was as if I had finally come home. I wanted to live there forever!

We ate huge bowls of steaming soup around a scarred wooden table. There were Hans and Fritz, Marta and Liesli. An old grandma sold colorful garments from a store on the ground floor of the ornate little chalet in which our family lived. Fragrant curls of wood covered a woodcarver's floor situated down a narrow stairway underneath the store. Accordion music filled the nights, and during the day a fountain splashed merrily outside my window. As I nestled down in an unbelievably soft feather-bed, tucked away in an attic with pull-down stairs, I felt more peace than I had ever known. But, one dark and rainy night we left, never to return. I cried as quietly as I could.

I remember almost nothing of the trip back to the States. Later, as I sat in our darkened front room, I stole glances at my father as he showed slides of our travels to his friends. He was so jovial and generous to them, but I was terrified of him. I had been taught to call him by his first name, never "Dad" or Daddy."

No matter how long I looked at him, I did not know him. His speech was heavily accented with German. He had immigrated to America as a young man in order to avoid the draft. A veterinarian by schooling, he never practiced the art as far as I know. Rather, he savagely beat our cocker spaniel with a rubber hose. Before I was even a teenager, my mother told me that he indulged in sodomy with animals. It was too much for me to comprehend. The horror of it went down inside of me and disappeared.

When I say I had a sister named Mimi, it's like looking at an anatomy book. I know I had a sister named Mimi. I know I have a spleen. It's a fact. Twelve years older than I, she lived with us until I was four years old, but I don't remember her during that time. I don't even remember myself during that time. She was a part of my mother's past, but not my father's. Also born out of wedlock, she lived on the fringes of our lives.

I start remembering her about the time we came home from Europe. She was beautiful, with dark hair and long eyelashes. We were opposites with my fine, blondish hair and blue eyes. Her eyes were the color of Chinese jade. She always smelled wonderful and dressed like a model. My little-girl clothes were crumpled and soiled. Somehow, though, I never wanted to imitate her. I only wished her favor. And she seemed to like me well enough. We even sunbathed together once in a while.

Mimi died when I was in my early twenties. I know now that we desperately needed each other, but neither one of us was capable of doing anything about it. The waxen face in her casket was that of a familiar stranger that I knew I had once loved.

By the time I was ten I was beginning to recognize that my world was somehow closed in. I sensed it more than anything else, and it made me wistful. A lot of the time I stayed in my bedroom just being bored. One afternoon I was sitting on my bed staring at a colorful story time linoleum that covered my floor. It had pictures of fairy tales and childhood rhymes. "Rub-a-dub-dub, three men in a tub"—I wanted to be involved with real people!

Going to my window, I peered across a narrow driveway to the silent, never-changing sameness of the house next door. Two-story like ours, its shade-drawn windows were grime laden and uninviting. My own windows were unwashed and screened, which made me feel claustrophobic in spite of the filmy pick-flowered curtains covering them. It was as if the two houses had argued years before and never made up.

I felt a sudden compulsion to visit an old woman who lived in this house so close to ours. It was a rare thing for Mom to let me go, but this time she did. Picking some small lawn daisies, I made my way to Old Woman's door and knocked. Her low, scraping voice called me in to where she sat in an ancient, over-stuffed rocking chair.

Her skin reminded me of a days-old, deflating balloon, and her fingernails were ridged like paper muffin cups. Her high-piled hair was so translucent I could see her colorless scalp underneath. Old Woman took my offering of daisies and held them to her nose as if they were roses. And then we talked—nobody talked to me at home! It was exhilarating, though I had a nagging feeling that I was doing something forbidden. Eventually she nodded off to sleep, letting her dentures drop to her chest. Brown with age, the sight of them gagged me. Slipping quietly away, I hoped that I'd never get that old, never have false teeth.

Back in my room, I felt distressed. Though it had gotten me

out of the house, my visit with Old Woman was not what I really wanted. I longed to play with the neighborhood kids at their houses. Mom allowed them to play with me as long as they came to *my* house, but I could never go to *theirs*. As a result, Mom offended several mothers, and no one came much anymore.

I didn't like being at home. The hatred my parents had for each other permeated the air. Mom, threatened and threatening fought back in ways meant to chill my father's blood. I remember her moving, shadowlike, to stand motionless behind my father as he watched TV, a heavy iron frying pan gripped white-knuckled in her hands. When my father became aware of her presence, he turned and looked at her. Whatever thoughts he had were unspoken. He deliberately resumed watching his program, eyes bulging slightly. After a while Mom quietly slipped away to replace the pan on the stove.

By the time I was twelve, the tension at home had reached the breaking point. Normality was a pretended veil we all wore. I desperately wanted to talk to Mom about what was happening. What *was* happening? Once I tried asking my brother, but he was preoccupied with television and shooed me away. Since we had outgrown fighting with teddy bears, we had little to do with each other.

Upstairs in my room I sought a refuge. Though I thought my square-shaped bedroom was the most boring in the house, it had a most wonderful closet! Tucked away under a slanting roof, it was narrow and deep, almost like a forgotten, little second room. Best of all, it had a window. Up high, I couldn't see anything out of it but the sky, but I loved the sky! I went to my closet, shut the door and looked up and out.

No screens transgressed its face. Though dirty, the window offered an honest, upward view. Hungry for a reality beyond my troubled existence, here I found solitude and privacy to cry. Reaching my fingers up toward the cold glass until they chilled, I pressed them against my eyelids until my heartache subsided.

Mom had told us for some time that she was determined to wait until my brother and I were legally old enough to choose in whose custody we wished to remain before she filed for divorce. We were both old enough, now, so she made her move. One day we were told that our father would be served papers the following afternoon. We would go into hiding the next morning.

That night, as I dangled my legs over the arm of a sofa, I watched my father repair a light switch in the dining room. An unanticipated sense of loss overwhelmed me. Though I feared this man exceedingly, I didn't want our home broken. Meager as it was, it was all the security I had. A surge of compassion swept over me for my father. He had no idea he was about to lose his family. Would he care?

I don't know you. Who are you, anyway? You are my father, but I have never called you that to your face. What is a father?—even the word makes me turn inside. You never speak to me. You only touched me once that I can remember. We were sitting in the car while Mom went in to get my brother from first grade. You slid your hand across the seat and under my dress. I didn't want you to touch me like that.

We fled the next day, a jumble of paper bags and schoolbooks, to a friend of Mom's. Her little apartment was full of torn furniture that stank. We stayed there several weeks. My brother and I had to sneak to school a block at a time, Mom in the lead watching for my father's old pink Nash. By the time we got there my stomach was churning. Taking the stairs two at a time, I rushed to a window where I could watch Mom until she was out of sight.

One morning I saw the Nash pull up next to her. She kept walking and disappeared around a corner. Panic cut my breathing to gasps. I didn't know what to do. Afraid to leave school, afraid of what might happen to Mom, I barely got through the day. When I got home, she was sitting in the kitchen reading, with a cigarette burning in an ashtray. She never mentioned the incident.

Unable to work through the extreme anxiety building inside of me, I started experiencing loss of memory at school. There were days I couldn't recall my locker combination and was reduced to spinning the dial, trying to *feel* the numbers. Sometimes I got it open in the morning but couldn't retrieve my lunch at noon. If I couldn't open it in the morning, I threw my lunch on top, often to return later to find it gone. Too humiliated to report my dilemma to anyone because I was afraid somebody would discover that I was abnormal, I suffered greatly from a growing lack of self-confidence.

It is very hazy now, but there was an English or government class that I had trouble finding. I still can't recall how it all turned out. I only remember leaning my back against a cement wall in a hallway and thinking how cold it was. I was sweating.

Sometimes my right hand went limp and I didn't have the strength to direct my pencil across my paper. Fear of reprisal from my teachers made me silent, while tears of panic and desperation were quickly dispersed into my sleeves.

Then the first hint of determination began to make its way into my heart. Steadying my right hand with my left, I fought back. I also learned to use my left hand in many ways and today remain fairly ambidextrous.

Eventually we moved back into our house. Stripped of much of our furniture, it looked like it had been raped. At least the old bear rug and the deer head were gone! Then Mom pulled all the curtains and drapes, shutting out the light. Day after day they stayed pulled. An awful sickness welled up inside of me. It was like we had all died and been buried. *Only, I'm alive!* my heart pleaded.

The curtains remained pulled for two years.

Chapter Three

With All Your Might

The day came for an official visit with my father, prior to custody proceedings. My brother and I were to meet with him separately in the presence of his lawyer. As I entered the room where he sat, I felt suffocated. He was as overweight and bald as ever; his face pinched into a smile. I sat down on a cool leather chair and involuntarily wet my pants. Near hysteria made me dizzy. This man facing me was a stranger! We had never talked—how were we to talk now?

His lawyer asked me if I wanted to see him on a regular basis. When I replied with an emphatic "No!" my father leaned forward and placed a new twenty-dollar bill on my knees. His eyes caressed me, ugly with exaggeration. Contempt scalded my heart. Bolting for the door, I turned only long enough to throw the crumpled money in his startled, furious face.

"Keep your money! Keep your dirty money," I screamed. I never saw him again.

I wish someone had asked me if I wanted to live in a house where there were no curtains! My mind began to expand into fantasies where light played a major part, and at night I dreamed about flying. I was able to fight the awful pull of gravity by the sheer strength of my heart's desires. Lifting into the air, I soared rapturously over high mountains and meadows that looked ever so much like Switzerland.

I begged Mom to let us open the drapes, but she was adamant. To her the drapes were our guardsmen. What she could not seem to grasp was that our home had become a virtual prison. When we got home from school she called from work every hour to make sure we were there. My brother succumbed to her demands and faded into a couch in front of the TV. I began spending more and more time in my closet. Looking up at my window, I crouched there crying, crying, crying—sure I was losing my mind.

Somehow, in all of my agony, my heart lurched toward God. One afternoon, though I knew only the possibility of His existence, I cried out to Him:

Oh God, if you exist please help me! I'm so scared. What's wrong with me? I can't remember my locker number. I forget where my classes are. Am I going crazy? I don't want to be crazy! I'm like a stranger to the kids at school. I hate being shut up in this house—it's a prison! I can't see outside. I want to see outside! I want to talk to somebody! I want to be normal!

Tiredness like that of Old Woman slowed my thinking. Curling up near the back of the closet, I pulled familiarity around me like a cloak to the wind.

Why am I praying to you? I'm not even sure you exist. Do you? Do you see me? Do you hear me? Do you care? I turned my face to the floor. *Help me! I don't want to live anymore!*

It was hard enough just being a teenager. Everyday life seemed simultaneously cosmic and microcosmic, explosive and implosive—then frustratingly inert. To be disciplined during these years I expected; to be isolated was devastating. I was shut away from everybody, forbidden to leave home. It felt like all my friends had boarded a train, hands waving in the sunshine, voices lifted in harmless sporting as they journeyed toward becoming. I pictured myself running as hard as I could alongside the tracks, unable to keep up. But I had to keep running because I knew I needed to get where they were going.

Lonesome and distraught, two years passed while I tried to fill the wrenching hole in my heart caused by my enforced isolation. But how do you fill that kind of hole—with television?

The twenty-one-inch peek at the outside world fascinated me, but continually reminded me of my prison. I took to sneaking into the back yard to climb a tree, getting up as high as I dared, even in the rain. There, little birds chirped and ants marched in columns as I gripped the rough bark with my legs. I had to keep touching life.

I wondered a lot about God as I listened to the wind thread musically through the leafy branches and brush across my face.

Mom's employment kept her away from home fourteen hours a day. When she returned she dropped onto a couch, drank some coffee, and fell asleep. Each morning she was gone before I left for school—except for the nights she went out. Then she left and was gone until early morning, returning only in time to change her clothes and leave for work. Those nights were the hardest. The house grew cold and spooky. I lay awake for hours listening to each board retire for the night.

Sometimes guys called, but I wasn't allowed to go out and I didn't want to sneak out. I was repelled by the thought of "running around." I made a decision: things were going to be different with me. Mom had been married at least three times that I knew of, and my sister's father hadn't been one of them. My sister had married too young and her marriage was in trouble. Even my grandmother had divorced. Whatever it took to make a difference, that's what I'd do. I wasn't sure what that something was, but I did know that sneaking out with boys late at night wasn't going to help.

All the housework fell to me, and I did it gladly. Making order out of things seemed the best activity I could think of. When I was small my mother used to tuck me in at night with a little rhyme:

Good night, sleep tight; wake up bright in the morning light,

To do what's right with all your might, good night, my sweetheart darling.

I loved it when she said those words to me—especially "sweetheart darling." I imagined that she really *did* love me to call me that. How I wanted her to love me! So now I was trying to do what was right with all my might.

One thing I was allowed to do was to shop for groceries, probably because Mom was simply too tired to do it herself. I did so with intensity. I bought only good things and tried to make the money go as far as I could. Mom opened cans. I decided to learn how to cook. I purchased seasonings with names I couldn't even pronounce and sprinkled them over everything. I discovered that un-soaked beans could boil for hours and remain inedible. The hard part was that everything was eaten in front of the TV. No one talked. No one noticed.

One night, with Mom asleep on the couch and my brother occupied with television, I slipped upstairs to my mother's room. A gifted woman, she had painted her bedroom walls with murals. Fantastic colors embodied fairytale Pan and wistful girls clothed with leaves and flowers, a whimsical frog sitting on a toadstool, a winking snail, cobwebs with dewdrops—it was all so wonderful! I tried to imagine such a happy world.

Going to a window, I opened it and knelt in the darkness. Outside was the real world. I could see the lights of the city. I could hear cars and the occasional bark of a dog. Mesmerized by the sounds of life, I leaned out as far as possible and felt my heartbeat in my stomach. I wanted to die, but I wanted so much to live!

Christmas season I turned sixteen. For hours I stared at our Christmas tree. It made the front room look like we were a happy family, and I wanted that very much. But I was always reminded of what we were. Reminded by Mom how awful Christmas used to be when our father lived with us—how awful he had made our lives.

Mom's face was grim with remembering. I wished she'd let go of the past, but she brought it forward almost daily, to contaminate our lives—like someone saving sour milk and pouring it into every fresh carton. And it wasn't just the misery of her life with our father. With deep sighs and biting remarks she went on to recall the general and specific failures of her own family and how glad we all should be that we didn't have to see any of them.

The truth was that Mom didn't like anybody. She had no friends that I ever knew of. Consequently, we never went anywhere or visited family. I wasn't even sure what my aunts and uncles looked like, I had seen them so rarely. Not that they lived so far away. The only person Mom spoke well of was Nonnie, my grandmother.

Nonnie.

I didn't see much of her, either; but the few memories of her were like the bright bachelor buttons she grew in her tiered flower gardens. In sharp contrast to Mom, Nonnie was cheerful and full of life. She was also a Christian, but I didn't know what that meant. She never said much about it to us, probably because Mom was so "disgusted" with "pious people." Yet, Nonnie managed to implant in my young mind the distinct understanding that the Bible was from God. It was like an appointment had been made deep inside of me: someday I would find out for myself.

That spring, one lazy Sunday (Mom worked Sundays) I could stand it no longer. I opened the front door and stood in a beam of sunlight that seemed to suck me right out of the house and into the early-morning air. Charged with desire for the freshness of grass and openness, I headed for a park only three houses away. Soon I was running on crunchy gravel along a path leading to a city girl's country.

I ran past a reservoir's glistening cascade of water that, when I was a little girl, I thought looked like a princess' gown. I passed fish ponds and flower gardens until I came to an expanse of lawn facing a bandstand. The grass sparkled with moisture. Huge maples moved gracefully in the wind. The sky spread extravagantly above me, frothy with high-flying cumulus clouds. Involuntarily, I shouted with joy!

I headed for a water tower. Two hundred steps encased in brick wound round and round to the top of the tank. I started climbing, stopping at each window-opening to take in the view.

There were no curtains here, not even glass! My heart felt like it was arching, like when I was flying in my dreams.

I was out of breath when I reached the top. It was almost too wonderful! From there I could see far into the distance, beyond the city to the mountains. Snowcapped peaks beckoned me. Gulls soared effortlessly on wind currents. Pressing my face against the cold iron bars that had been placed there to keep people from falling, my thoughts turned to my mother's religion. It was an odd mixture of horoscopes, omens, and mystical ideas. I was not invited to understand or share her faith. When she did mention God she said "He," so I thought of God as male, kind of.

We had taken confirmation classes at an Episcopal church during my parents' divorce because Mom thought it would help the judge decide in her favor in the custody proceedings. The most I got out of it was a little potted marigold on Easter morning. It looked pretty, but didn't smell so good. *Maybe religion is like that*, I thought.

I remembered a great cathedral I'd seen in Europe as a child. Somehow I had gotten the idea that God lived there, at least some of the time. Everything was so immense, so heavy and old, so beautiful in a touch-me-not sort of way. I had felt very reverent there. Something inside me wanted to stay, yet something else wanted to run.

Standing at the top of the water tower I felt strangely drawn to God. Why? Was it because I had always thought of Him as *up* and now I was high above the treetops? How did one ever find God, anyway? I'd read once that the Jews were God's chosen people. If only I'd been born Jewish! It didn't seem fair—but not much did.

With one long, hungry look at the far mountains I turned and began my descent, noting the lonely, hollow sound of my feet on the steep metal staircase. Outside again, I marveled at how full of fragrances the warm air was. Wandering off a pathway onto the grass, I stretched out on my stomach next to some flowers and peeked underneath their fair crowns. The view was enchanting! Pretty little pebbles were spotted with lace-like shadows from the petals above. It was so very peaceful and right. If only all of life were like this, I mused.

As I lay on the soft green grass, I realized I felt far more at home with plants than I did with people. I related to their strong, living stems that stretched upward toward the sun. It was almost as if they grew for the joy of it! Why did nature seem happy, when it could not think, and people who could, were so miserable?

Had I ever been truly happy? I tried to remember, but it was as if someone had pulled undeveloped film prematurely out of a camera, leaving the exposed strip blank. Why had so much of my life been erased from my mind? I remembered only snatches here and there.

Tears welled up in my eyes as I concentrated.

A cow had chased me once—where was I when it happened? In fifth grade I shinned up a tether pole to attach a ball because a little boy with me could not—but who was my teacher? I couldn't remember any of my classmates either. And whatever happened to fourth grade? And third? And before that?

There was something worse. I sensed my understanding was somehow impaired, as if someone had scissored away part of my brain. I knew I wasn't stupid. School had always come easily. It was a different part of me, deep inside that lay disconnected and unsure.

It was too much to deal with that lovely sunny Sunday.

I got up and consciously filled my lungs with the same air that made the sky so piercingly blue. As the sounds of the park filled my mind, I decided to run, to let my feet argue with life while my brain simply went along for the ride.

Chapter Four

The Beginning of Hope

God's voice is in this world. It echoes in the songs of meadowlarks and mingles with the music of streams. The wind is its carriage, and stillness its veil. And so the human heart is wooed by the Infinite. But only as the written Word of God is heard can the resonance of His voice become knowledge to our soul.

I was a junior in high school and my only social outlets were school choir performances and an occasional church dance. I didn't have a date for the dances. I was escorted by a motherly girlfriend who had convinced Mom that she'd watch me like a hawk. It was fun, but I was never sure just how to act, and was always glad when the lights were dimmed. Feeling less conspicuous, I relaxed enough to be swept away by soft music, held in the arms of an attending young man. I was always home by 11:00 p.m.

Our choir performances took us all over the city. We'd pack ourselves, snacks and laughter, into a bus and leave school late Friday afternoon to sing before kind old ladies and their gentlemen, or some group of finely dressed professionals who clapped fingers to palms as we bowed in unison from the risers. Our choirmaster was crippled by polio, but led us magnificently. I felt good about our performances and sang freely, a part of the whole. Music filled my heart as I hid among the faces of my classmates.

Choirmaster suggested that we volunteer for extra credit by

singing in his church choir on Sundays. Since his church was within walking distance from where I lived, I decided to go. I had been sneaking out regularly Sunday mornings, anyway, to go to the park. The thought of singing in church greatly appealed to me. Since Choirmaster explained to us that we weren't expected to stay for the service, I never did.

Words of praise were in my mouth about a God I did not know, and my hunger for Him was becoming uncomfortable. About the same time, my mother actually let me spend a few weekends with a Jewish girl I knew from school. I was thoroughly surprised at this freedom, but gladly made the best of it. We attended synagogue on Saturday morning, then played tennis in the afternoon. I felt wonderful!

My Jewish friend had a very closely-knit family that I found culturally exciting. There was an emotional pull to their music and manner of speech, almost like a memory begging to be free. Without trying, I fit in. But something was missing: their God was screened off. Messiah had become tradition rather than hope. The throb of their existence generations ago was now only faintly pulsating. It was as if there was nothing left for me.

Singing in Choirmaster's church choir no longer satisfied me. The singing of praise words left empty parentheses in my soul. Often, after leaving the service, I walked to a cemetery adjacent to the park. There I wandered among the headstones, feeling as detached from life as the cold marble upon which the names were inscribed. What had these no-longer-people known about life? They had lived and died and taken their secrets with them.

Somehow, I pictured them all buried face down. Even so, I felt quieted. A sense of settledness hung over the place. It was like starting at an ending. I had found a human boundary and was working myself back. Maybe, in the process, I could make some sense out of my chaotic world. The process gave me a feeling of hope, even though the weight of my loneliness was like a gravestone in my belly.

One afternoon a new student strolled into my creative writing class. The only seat available was the one directly behind mine. Before the week ended we were friends. He soon introduced me to his sister, and it was a great day when the three of us realized we lived only blocks away from each other. What excited me most, however, was how openly they both talked about God—like He was their Friend! They told me that God's Son, Jesus Christ, was coming back to earth to take those who believed in Him to heaven to live with God forever.

His sister talked about Christ, but I was too embarrassed to tell her how repulsed I had been by the crucifix as a child. I'd seen them in European homes, surrounded by faded and dusty artificial flowers. To me, Christ was a religious artifact that had little to do with my yearning for God. But I was intrigued, and when she invited me to attend church with them, I immediately agreed to go.

I had a dream the night before. All the kids in my neighborhood had gathered with me in my front yard. A large hand came down from the sky and a wonderful, deep voice invited us to climb on. It was God's hand! I pulled myself up and onto His hand and was immediately filled with joy such as I had never before known. The others did not join me and eventually left. I awoke feeling terribly disappointed to find myself still in bed.

Still a bit melancholy, I went along to church with my new friends, and soon the newness of everything swept away any thoughts of the night before. I couldn't help but notice how comfortable everyone seemed with his or her Bible. During a study period, in a class that met in a choir loft, the Scriptures were used as naturally as I might use one of my school textbooks. For the first time I heard and read words that changed my life forever. When we knelt to pray, I opened my eyes and looked out over the sanctuary. In a moment everything blurred. These were God's people praying! Old women, young men, and children—they were all there. It was a sacred place, and I was there too—all of me. I was in His hand!

I took Bible studies twice a week that month and read everything given to me by their kind minister. What I read charged me with hope. I began a book on the life of Christ, carrying it with me to read every chance I got. As His life opened up before me, I was filled with awe. No dusty artifact was He, but a Carpenter and a Leader of men—a real Person who held children and ate dinner with people others avoided.

When I finished the chapter on the crucifixion I put the book down, stunned. Such a cloud came over me that I could barely concentrate on my lessons at school. For two weeks I grieved silently. It was too private to put into words. I had grown to love Him. To see Him treated so cruelly and then slain so pitilessly was more than my heart could stand. In my closet I cried out my sorrow. It was all so unfair!

At last I picked up the book and began to read again. Within a few pages I came to the story of the resurrection. I remember the moment well. At first I was dumbfounded. Could such a thing as this really *be*? And then the joy hit. Laughter escaped my throat like runaway children, free and uninhibited, my legs following suit as I leaped through the house shouting, "He's alive! He's alive!" Nothing else mattered anymore. I had seen into heaven! The awful emptiness of my life was filled. I was baptized the following weekend, just one month short of my seventeenth birthday.

Many warm hands touched me, admitting me into the family of God. How my spirit drank of their welcome! I was forgiven and washed clean by the blood of the Lamb. Though I was not sure what horrible crimes I had committed, I accepted this much as I had always accepted the blame when my brother and I got into trouble. Whatever it meant, I knew that Jesus loved me enough to suffer the abuse of Calvary. For that, He had my fiercest loyalty.

Only one thing gave me pause: God was addressed as "Father." Though outwardly I understood and accepted such terminology and dutifully prayed the Lord's Prayer along with everyone else, I could not bring myself to use this expression when praying privately. Not that I deliberately avoided it. It just never came out of my mouth. Sometimes, if I ran the words all together, "Dearfatherinheaven," I could manage it because it was wrapped in the cellophane of religious rote. Mostly, I just said, "God."

After my prayer patterns were established, this unconscious suppression became the norm, and I didn't think much more about it. Jesus was the easy part. Getting close to the Father was another matter. After all, He only accepted me because I was hidden in Christ. It was almost like Christ was there to protect me from the Father. Now, *that* was familiar ground!

I accepted "God is love" and "God so loved the world…" To me it meant that God was willing to let me live in heaven someday if I was obedient to His will. I was to do what was right with all my might and be thankful I had a chance to live forever. It was almost generic. In a sea of repenting sinners, I was allowed entrance to heaven. It was the best of love I had known. At last I was being permitted!

I tried very hard to be good. I had never wanted to be bad, anyway, so it wasn't like life was going to be terribly different, except that now there were edges and corners in my world. The insipid aimlessness that had left my existence so undefined had been replaced by a rock-solid goal: I wanted to be with Jesus.

Other things changed, too. I ate dinner with believers in their homes and learned how to make conversation at a table. I went walking with them along wooded trails and learned the casualness of sociability. They took me skiing. I leaned into their normality and willed myself to be like them. Mom fought my association with them at first, but gave up out of her perpetual tiredness.

I took my brother with me as often as he would go, but he never seemed to have the drive that I did. It was as if I was scaling the fences, then opening the gate for him to go through. If the gate wasn't open, he just sat down. Though he was fourteen months older, I came to think of him as my younger brother.

If only all of this could have filled the deficit of my upbringing!—but it could not. Outwardly, I eased into a much-needed frame of reference. Inwardly I had no idea of the workings of a successful family life. My concept of love was stunted and faulty. My concept of myself was almost non-existent. I lived to please others, never considering that it might be just as right for others to please me. The Bible seemed to echo my own heart: I was undeserving and unworthy. Already stripped of much of my personhood, it was easy to assume that this was the context of Christianity.

My feet were set to walk a long and heartbreaking road.

Chapter Five

One Hundred Miles Away

Mom wanted to get away. She was being worn down by her fear of my father. My brother graduated from high school and took up residence on the end of a couch. It was summer again, and I had just returned from visiting some friends across state. They suggested that Mom sell the house and relocate in their city. They would help.

Mom grabbed at the chance. Taking what she could get from the sale of our house, we crated our things and moved to Small-Town.

Our new apartment was on the very edge of the city, facing nowhere. Sitting on the top of the stairs at night, for the first time in my life I actually heard silence! The air was free from city contaminants and felt life giving as it greeted my face. Tumbleweed scratched aimlessly along, congregating under the stairway. It was my senior year in high school.

Mom worked sporadically, caring for a child in our apartment complex. Without a car, our family was stranded. Fortunately, the school I attended was within walking distance. I had an early morning accelerated class and found it delightful to move along the sleepy morning streets. The sky was often the color of tangerine sherbet, and the air carried on it the taste of the golden grasses lying languid and dry against stone-hard dirt. My brother remained in place on his end of the couch.

We were poor. With permission from a school counselor I

took two jobs, leaving school early to go to one of them. It was called babysitting, but the "baby" was a sixteen-year-old ox-sized teenager with a paper route. Since he was never home, I was told to busy myself doing laundry, cleaning the house, and preparing the evening meal—all for fifty cents an hour! We needed the money so badly that I did it anyway. I got home after dark, having run full throttle across a vacant lot near our apartment complex, singing at the top of my lungs, "Take the name of Jesus with you, child of sorrow and of woe."

I lost the job quite by accident. Mom never taught me how to cook. What little I knew I had taught myself by trial and error. One day the lady of the house left instructions about a pot roast she wanted me to prepare for the evening meal. Her instructions were precise: "Put the roast into the electric frying pan to brown; then cover it and place it in the oven at 350°."

I did exactly as instructed, wondering at the time how to balance the legs of the electric frying pan on the oven grates. The next morning, my counselor called me into her office. She was doubled over with laughter. The plastic parts on the frying pan had melted, I had been fired, and, in the process, the school had found out about the babysitting sham.

"It serves her right!" the counselor grinned. Then she hired me herself to do housework at the going rate.

I was eighteen now, and Mom said little about my comings and goings. I spent long weekends with friends on a farm a long way into the nowhere I so loved. I could scarcely believe the expanse of the night sky. Lying on top of a huge stack of hay bales, I felt flattened out by the canopy of stars overhead.

Dear God, it's all so beautiful! I can hardly take it in! Even though I don't have a dress or shoes for graduation, I feel rich! I want to go to college. I want to live for you. How I wish Mom understood. She doesn't seem to care what I think about anything. I give her all my money. I wish she would let me love her.

Graduation night one of the guys from my church asked me what I wanted to do. I told him to drive me one hundred miles away from SmallTown—a symbolic flight into the future. We drove two hours until his odometer registered that we had gone the hundred miles. We were in the middle of nowhere. I got out and walked a short distance away, asking him to remain behind. In the moonlight I saw the outline of a distant ridge. The air was pleasant. For some reason, I could not pray. I was too full of words to single them out into the pattern of speech. Swollen with dreams for the future, I stood in the quiet, living.

My friend called softly, asking if I was all right. As I came toward the car, he mentioned casually that he had sleeping bags in the trunk. Though I would have loved to sleep outside, I didn't want to spend the night with him and suggested we start back—it was really late. He shrugged his shoulders, and we got back in the car. When he turned on the engine, the headlights startled a rabbit with long ears.

Life surrounds us, I thought. *I wonder how much more there is that I never see.* We drove back in silence. Two weeks later I left home, never to return. I was joining a girl across the state for the summer to sell books door-to-door in order to earn the money to enroll in a Christian college that fall.

Indeed, my education was about to begin. How little did I know the price I would pay for it! My heart was filled with dreams, but I was about to walk into grief and tragedy that would bring me down to the depths of despair. There I would learn about my humanness. I would crawl on my belly until no trace of my old ways of thinking remained. And slowly, more slowly than I would ever have allowed, I would be reborn.

It was all hidden from me that day as, with one medium-sized suitcase, I boarded a northbound train. Settling into a seat by the window, I watched the countryside, which seemed to ignore us as we passed by. The seat next to me was vacant. Then I heard a voice.

"'Scuse me," he slurred, "'s this seat taken?"

His bloodshot eyes barely acknowledged my presence as he dumped himself into place next to me. Falling immediately into a guttural slumber, his head came to rest on my arm. The stench of sour liquor blew in my face. Turning away, I felt hot tears slip from under my eyelids. Panic welled inside of me—panic from too many years seeing my father drunk, too many memories wanting to be forgotten.

It seemed forever before the train made a station stop. Jarred awake, the man next to me got up and headed for a restroom. Leaning back against the seat, I closed my eyes. I hadn't even had time to think of praying when a crisply dressed matron slid into the seat next to me.

"I'll just sit here," she said softly. "You poor dear! I saw him heading for you. Well, he can just find somewhere else to sit!"

Soon the train was on its way, and we chatted pleasantly off and on for the remainder of the trip. Just before I took my leave, she reached out and held my hand.

"God be with you! You're a sweet young woman. I'll be praying for you."

I wonder if she did. Somebody needed to!

Mimi met my train. Lively and beautiful, she never stopped talking. She had remarried recently and seemed quite happy. I spent the next few days with her and her husband in their home. Her tastes ran to black lacquered furniture, Japanese art, and little candles that floated in water. Her first husband had been Catholic; her second was Jewish.

It was odd, yet delightful, being with my sister. She fussed over my hair and told me dirty jokes that I didn't understand. Her husband's family was predictably large, and she obviously reveled in their customs and outings. Her evening dresses were satin and low cut, and her perfume came in tiny bottles with foreign names. I got the feeling that there was a good deal of tribal competitiveness involved, and wondered if she was truly as happy as she appeared to be.

The day came for me to be dropped off at the house where I was to spend the summer. We drove by it the first time. It was so dingy that Mimi hesitated to leave me there, but not knowing what to do with me if she didn't, she pulled into the driveway and began saying goodbye before I even got out of the car. I walked up to the door and knocked. My partner with whom

I would spend the summer in this new book-selling adventure opened the door, and I waved Mimi back into her own life.

Partner greeted me with gushes of "I'm-so-glad"s and drew me into the house. Steering me through a dumpily furnished front room, she deposited me out on the patio in back. There I met my new "family"—two gangly teenage boys and "Mama" and "Papa." Flies crawled on a table among fruit and open jars of peanut butter and jelly. Partner offered to show me our room.

It was a small room just off the bathroom, crammed full of boxes of what looked like Salvation Army castoffs. Sagging bunk beds were shoved against a curtained window.

"Top or bottom?" queried my jovial friend.

Taking in the narrow space underneath the top bunk and Partner's rather abundant figure, I said I thought it'd be fun to sleep on top. She quickly agreed, adding that she'd feel better not having to crawl up there since there was no ladder.

When I asked about a closet, she informed me that it was full. We had to keep our things in our suitcases. *Oh well*, I thought, *I have little enough, and we'll be gone most of the time anyway.* We planned long days and early nights.

Shutting the bedroom door, Partner's face took on a new seriousness.

"There's no latch on the bathroom door," she whispered. "I prop a chair underneath the doorknob. It's the only way to insure privacy. Papa wanted daughters all his life, and he's very solicitous. He'll offer to wash your back if he knows you're taking a bath. I'm sure he means well," she finished weakly.

Quickly her bubbly self again, she led me back out to the patio where we spent the rest of the afternoon talking about the Bible.

It took me three days to work up the courage to bathe. By this time Papa had told me many times how wonderful it was to have "his girls" at last; a real answer to prayer. Mama didn't say much. She seemed more interested in the poodles she was raising—ten of them. You had to be careful where you stepped!

When their oldest son took a fancy to me, Mama's prayers

seemed in the process of being answered too. She was forever sending me with him to the store. I think she bought her groceries one at a time that summer. Fortunately, the young man was so timid that all he ever did was sneak looks at me. I think he would have passed out if I had taken the matter seriously.

His friend was a different matter. Chinese, he had graduated from college that spring and was staying temporarily with the family. Ten years older than I, he decided I needed someone to take care of me.

"You'll love Singapore!" he assured me.

He was to return to his homeland at the end of the summer and wanted to take me with him. Things were getting confusing again. It seemed like I was always ducking. If I wasn't careful, Singapore trapped me in a small hall between the kitchen and family room and pressed his petitions and kisses on me.

On another occasion I forgot to fix the chair in the bathroom when I went to take a bath. Fortunately I was slow in getting started and was still fully clothed when Papa burst in. He seemed as disappointed as I was relieved.

"I think I hear Mama calling you!" I said as I darted for my room.

I skidded on a wet floor just as I dashed through my doorway. Those dogs!

Tossing restlessly in my bunk that night, I wondered how in the world all this could be God's will for me? How did anybody know for sure what God wanted, anyway? I read my Bible every day, but it didn't say anything about the situation I was in. I wanted so much to obey Him. Someone had told me it was a sin to be discouraged, that it showed lack of faith, so I tried very hard to be cheerful, even when I prayed. But inside me, panic was building.

Chapter Six

Can This Be Happening?

The book-selling business wasn't going well at all. I gave away more books than I sold. People were so needy. It was fast becoming apparent that there would be no scholarship for me. I was worn down emotionally and staggering spiritually. Not that I had lost any of my first love for Jesus. He just seemed so far away and busy somewhere else in the universe.

Mid-July the guy who had driven me a hundred miles away from SmallTown showed up. He had gotten pretty intense before I left, and I wasn't very happy to see him. He asked me to go for a ride with him "just for old times." Not knowing what else to do, I went.

We drove to the edge of town and down a winding road that ended up in a garbage dump. I had never seen a garbage dump before. This one was huge. We kept going until we reached some trees. Hundred Miles stopped the car. Turning to me, he proposed. I was startled, and didn't answer at first. When he reached to pull me to him, I resisted.

"I want to go to college," I told him. "I want to get an education."

"You can read all the books you want," he offered. "But on the farm you won't need any college degree. My mom does just fine. She's happy as pie."

The thought of spending the rest of my life on a farm did not excite me, especially with someone I didn't even love. I tried to turn him down as politely as I could. He became insistent, then angry.

"If you won't marry me, you can just get out and walk home!" It was getting dark.

"Please, just take me home," I begged, helplessness rolling over me like a sheet of chilled water. He reached across me and opened the car door on my side.

"It's your decision," he growled. I got out and started walking.

"Hey! Where do you think you're going?" he yelled after me. "Get back in the car!"

Crying hard, I told him I'd rather walk a hundred miles than get back into the car with him. I walked the distance out, his headlights on my back while he pleaded and apologized. Finally reaching a gas station, I called my "family." Hundred Miles left before they got there.

The next afternoon Mama came out to where I was sitting on the patio, her face crayon-white. In a halting voice, she explained that Hundred Miles had been killed in an automobile accident. The highway patrol called because my phone number had been found on his body.

I pitched forward sobbing.

"I told him I hoped I'd never see him again, but I didn't want him to die! Please, I didn't want him to die!"

For the next few hours I went from room to room crying. I felt like I had killed Hundred Miles. Partner kept asking me, kind of stating it, "Then, you *did* love him?"

After a while Mama came to me again, her eyes glassy. Her words hit me like buckshot.

"It's him. He's on the phone! He's not dead! It's all a big story. He wanted to find out if you loved him."

I had to make sure. Running to the phone, I screamed into the mouthpiece, "Is it *you*?"

When I heard his voice, I did not wait to hear what he was

saying. I hurled the phone across the room. It smashed into the fireplace. Someone grabbed me, but I pulled away and ran out of the house.

Nearby, under a passing freeway, a little stream ran through a culvert. I had often walked there to be alone. Instinctively, I headed there. Soon Mama and Singapore flanked me on both sides.

"No! No!" I kept screaming, but they pulled me down.

Sending Singapore back to the house. Mama tried to calm me.

"You have to understand men," she started.

The fight went out of me. Understand men? Would I ever understand anything!

Not more than a week after that I met another young man. A friend of Partner's, he was selling books in a nearby city. I had never met anyone so intense and deeply religious. His eyes seemed to look through me as we talked. Soon he was completely focused on me. He was a few years older than I, and I felt flattered, if not a little awed.

Within a few days he asked me to go for a walk with him, saying that he had something very important to tell me. We walked to the culvert and sat down on a log by the stream. He had his Bible with him, which he left open as he talked. Recounting the story of Jacob and Rebekah, he told me that he had been praying that God would bring him a wife as in the days of the patriarchs. I was his Rebekah, the girl God had given him to marry.

Compared to the household in which I was living, he seemed sane. I was convinced he was utterly sincere. He wasn't asking me; he was sharing with me the will of God for my life. As I listened to him, I felt a sense of relief. I was so tired; I had no money. I felt so lost, and he was so sure. He probably *did* know what God wanted. I certainly didn't.

We were married three weeks later. I wore a borrowed gown and stood in a stranger's front room with strangers as my attendants. I was not in love; I was in submission.

The whole affair seemed to be happening in slow motion.

Someone played a violin, and people kept hugging me. We left to attend a religious meeting. Then we went home to our little upstairs bedroom, our part of a house that we would share with another newly married couple. They got the downstairs with the kitchen and bathroom. Our "kitchen" was in the next building, behind a bakery where we would work. I can't even remember, now, where our bathroom was.

It was an awkward moment. We had said our vows and now we stood together, alone, in this unfamiliar room. Our clothes hung side by side in the narrow, doorless closet. My little bouquet of flowers lay wilting on the nightstand. Only one thing remained.

This stranger, who was now my husband, faced me.

"Take off your clothes and get into bed," he said simply.

I must have looked mortified, because he laughed and left the room.

My face burned and my fingers seemed double their size as I undid my garments. Quickly slipping into a pretty negligee that someone had thoughtfully supplied, I hesitated only briefly, then yanked a light cord hanging from a bulb in the center of the room. Diving for shelter under the covers, I felt far colder than the August night should have allowed.

Returning to a darkened room, my husband remarked off-handedly, "Oh, you turned out the light." The bed made horrible creaking noises as he joined me. "You might as well take that off," he said. "It'll only get in the way."

Mechanically, I discarded my gown. At least it was dark. Maybe, if I didn't have to say anything, he wouldn't notice that I was crying. What was wrong with me?

When he began kissing my mouth roughly, I was almost overwhelmed with panic. Only moments later, it became evident that there could be no consummation that night.

Disappointed, and a little peeved, he turned his back to me and went to sleep. All I could do was repeat the name of God, over and over and over. My mind blanked.

The following night was no better. My husband was very frustrated. "What's wrong with you?" he demanded, switching the light back on to read his Bible.

I began to wonder if I was normal.

By the third night, I could no longer hold in my torment. I put my head in his lap and cried so hard it felt as if my rib cage was going to explode. But he had already decided what needed to be done. Taking a towel, he covered my mouth and forced his way.

"Try not to make so much noise!" he said firmly when I became hysterical. "It has to be done. You'll enjoy this someday."

What he said had no meaning for me. I had decided to die.

Night after night, after each new ordeal, I lay in bed ridged, each heartbeat sending a shudder through my soul. I could hear the deep sounds of nocturnal life outside. No gentle sounds, these, but wild and haunting.

The bakery was located on an Indian reservation, and in the night came the rhythmic throb of distant chants. I wondered what they were doing, poor creatures. Day by day they came to beg moldy bread from the store, their faces expressionless. Their leathery cheeks seemed chiseled. Too noble to permit condescension, they asked forthrightly. It was dignity hung with rough blankets and adorned by carved beads and brightly colored taffeta.

Somehow, I understood. These were people who loved, feared, hoped, and then just existed—resignation sidled up against clouded nobility. Perhaps it could be so for them, I thought ruefully, because they could remember their rich heritage. Maybe that's what they did so deep in the night. They remembered with their chants and fires and strange rituals. Did they feel as haunted as they sounded? I could almost have felt a part of them, except that there were no memories for me to soothe away my beggarliness.

As I lay in bed each night listening, another sound came through the darkness, first throbbing, then crescendoing into a gnashing roar, screaming its warning into the blackness. Sometimes I could see the wide beam of its roving eye as it sent light 'round and 'round in the sky. Each time it passed, I could almost feel its churning steel wheels tearing my body apart against the tracks. Perhaps if I were deliberate enough there would be nothing left. It would be as though I had never been. Yes, one night I would simply walk away into forever.

One day I was headed for the kitchen when I heard a man's voice.

"We just want you to know we know," he said. I stopped and looked up. It was the young man from downstairs.

"We've heard you crying. We hear how roughly he speaks to you. If there is anything we can do..."

So. They'd heard us after all!

"...anything we can to do help?" he finished with a look of helplessness playing across his face.

Inside I cried out, go away! You don't know! *Oh God, please, where are you? Somebody, hold me! I need somebody to hold me!* I turned to the young man.

"Thanks, but it's okay. I'm all right."

It was a lie. Were my eyes as empty as my heart?

Later that day the owner of the bakery approached me. Taking me into his little office, he counseled me to learn a woman's place in marriage. It would help me adjust better, he assured me, and God would bless me with a long life.

Just what I wanted!

I wondered about *his* marriage. He slept apart from his wife, out in a screened shed. "For my health," he explained to anybody who had the nerve to ask.

His wife was the next to seek me out. A gracefully aging woman with a gentle demeanor, she was the one who handed out bread to the Indian women who came with their huge-eyed children. She was thanked with toothless grins as she reached out to touch the babies, often slipping small treats into their little hands.

"Come up to the house," she offered. "I want to show you something."

Whatever she showed me I have long forgotten. But as she

reached out to me, I felt my detachment from reality begin to crack, like leathery old skin.

"Something is terribly wrong," she probed delicately. "You need someone to understand, don't you? Not just to know, but to understand."

She continued talking softly to me. She did not intend to let me out of her sight.

"I'm afraid you are thinking of doing something desperate."

Had I been that transparent? Suddenly I felt sick. Putting my face down against my knees, I dug my knuckles into my eyes, trying to halt the tidal wave of tears that were falling.

"Mommy!"

Oh, how stupid to call Mommy! Why do I do that? She's not there. She's never been there. No one is there.

Oh God, I'm sorry! Please let me go!

She was holding me now, rocking me and stroking my hair. Knowing. Understanding, at least, that I was an empty-handed child. And when I was spent, she laid my head upon a taffeta pillow, and I slept. When I awoke she was still there. For the next few days, she always seemed to be there. Slowly, I turned back into life.

Turning back hurts. It means you feel again. Yet for me it also meant I could pray again. Not like before, but I did pray. Going out into the woods, I prayed with my eyes, tracing the border of green against the sky. I noticed the scent of wetness in the leaves and heard the birds and the wind. Tasting the freshness and calm of fall, I wrapped my arms around the trunk of a tree and prayed by just being.

My mind was still in such a paralyzed state that I could not formalize my thoughts into a recognizable prayer. Just the same, I communed with my Maker, perhaps not unlike a tree: created and Creator. I went as often as I could and lingered as long as I dared—the tree and God and I in a strange, healing embrace.

Slowly, as I began to get my bearings, I sensed that God was speaking directly to me, though I couldn't fully understand what He was telling me. I could only hear the water song and the wind chorus. But somehow, as I had prayed without words, so I began to "hear" without sounds. My heritage was greater than the Indians'. I belonged to the family of God. And mine was the Bread of Life, fresh from the throne of Grace.

Chapter Seven

Secrets in the Wind

My husband told me that God would hold us accountable someday for what we could have learned from the Bible and didn't. He studied constantly and wrote all of his ideas out on three-by-five cards, which he indexed alphabetically in a long metal file. The file sat on his desk like a verdict. I felt condemned whenever I thought about his cramped writing covering both sides of most of the cards. He hinted that I had better follow suit, but it was difficult for me to study the Bible and write like that. The metal file was sterile and cold, like his heart.

Saintman expected strict obedience from me, and he remonstrated with me severely if I faltered in the slightest. What I felt, or what I might think, was of no importance to him. His words scalded my heart.

Was God like that?

Rebelliousness stirred deeply within me, but was quickly replaced with chagrin. God had paid the price of Calvary for me. I belonged to Him. I should be grateful; it was a sin not to be. Saintman said so, many times.

Employment at the bakery lasted only three months. Our employers found Saintman to be incorrigible. We moved to a nearby town where he got work at a lumberyard, painting huge wooden spools. I spent my days in a dingy, second-story apartment located literally on the other side of the tracks. Each time a train passed, only twenty feet from our back bedroom, the whole building shuddered. It made me cringe.

I felt like I was being stalked by a demon of despair. The train became a symbol of all that was destructive in my life. I had barely decided to live but, as the days passed, I began to fight for life. Since I could not keep the train away, I defied it. Standing in the middle of our apartment, I refused to cringe. Drawing in a deep breath, I screamed back at its deafening roar.

"No!"

Every cell in my body seemed to scream, "No!"

Several times the train and I did battle. Then one day I'd had enough. Breaking off in the middle of my defiant scream, I rushed toward the bedroom window and yanked the curtain aside so violently that the whole thing, brackets and all, fell to the floor. There before me, on the other side of the dirty glass, a streak of red, blue, and silver thundered by. I could see it glistening in the rain. It was a passenger train, just an ordinary train. Its commonness struck me. I had won.

Though I longed for the out-of-doors, I could not bring myself to leave the apartment. An assortment of bedraggled and dirty men filled the street below. Discarded whiskey bottles with brown paper sacks twisted up around their necks littered the sidewalk. The warning to the unwary hung heavy in the air.

One afternoon, I heard a scuffling noise and then a woman cried out. Her voice, muffled and sobbing, pleaded with her attackers. I heard them drag her through our downstairs hallway. I cringed, knowing that if I went to her rescue, I, too, would be raped.

We had no telephone. I could not bear the sounds of her agony, and began banging furniture against the floor of our apartment. The building became silent. Gathering courage, I threw open our door and stomped into the hall. A vertical rectangle of daylight fell through an empty entrance. I cried most of that day.

A few days later, Bakery Woman came for a visit. She was

appalled at our living conditions and immediately offered me re-
employment at the bakery. Saintman could commute to work.
And so it was that we moved back, but only for a few months.
Saintman was fired from the lumberyard. During the next year
and a half, he went from one job to another taking us the length
of the state. Then, late one spring, he joined the Forest Service
for a six-month stint.

We took up solitary residence in an ugly canvas tent pitched
in the wilderness. At first I relished the idea of camping. City-
reared, I found it an exquisite release from cement and strung-
up wires. I was alone during the day while Saintman was on
duty. Having no sense of direction, I never wandered very far
from our campsite, but I reveled nonetheless in the gentle murmur of the woodlands. Fascinated by the extravagant variety of
plant life, I felt as if the brush of a master was painting an inner
canvas in my being.

Saintman warned me that bears and cougars lived in the
mountains, so I became uneasy when we moved camp to higher
country. The first time I heard a cougar scream, I thought it was
a woman. Saintman just laughed and said he hoped one didn't
get me. From that time on, my simple pleasure of dwelling in
the forest was tinged with apprehension.

On two occasions, Saintman used my fear of wild animals to
punish me. The first time happened after we drove his pickup to
the end of an old logging road to watch the sun set. For no apparent reason, he ordered me out of the truck. When I shut the
door, he drove off, leaving me alone in the fast-falling darkness.
Panicking, I ran after the truck, pleading for him to stop, but his
taillights disappeared around a bend in the road, and soon even
the roar of his pickup faded away. Out of breath and crying, I
slowed to a walk.

Suddenly I stopped. Someone was watching me! My skin
prickled. I started to run again, when I heard something running along side me in the woods to my right. When I ran it ran,
and when I stopped it stopped.

At first I thought it was Saintman, and called to him. Then a chilled awareness swept over me. I don't know how I knew—it wasn't Saintman. I had no choice but to keep running. Then I heard a cougar scream. Whether it was close or far away, I did not know.

All at once the lights from Saintman's pickup flooded the road. I raced forward. Reaching the truck, I grasped the door handle but didn't have enough strength to open it. Saintman did not stop the truck entirely, forcing me to trot alongside as I tried desperately with both hands to open the door. When I finally managed it, I was shaking so violently I almost couldn't climb in.

Saintman was laughing. As we drove back to camp he warned me that I'd better "shape up" or he'd leave me out there again.

He never bothered to tell me what I had done that angered him.

Another time Saintman left me alone in the tent most of one night. Terrified, I cried until I was sick. I could not comprehend being abandoned so ruthlessly. What could I have possibly done to deserve such treatment?

It was hard for me to turn to God for help, because Saintman claimed God and could quote dozens of scriptures to support his actions. I felt I had no basis to question him. I knew little enough of ordinary life, let alone about God or the Bible. Even so, when I cried, I cried God's name.

When Saintman returned he "comforted" me by having sex. As I watched the sunrise through my swollen eyes, I felt much like a little dog Saintman told me he owned when he was a child. He used to "punish" the dog so that he could comfort it later. He liked the way the dog acted when it "forgave" him. I pictured the dog crawling on its belly to Saintman. Poor little creature.

Sometime in the middle of the winter we moved several states away to a commune of "believers." At the time I was excited because I was so hungry for the company of other Christians. Saintman never talked to me much, and I was starving for conversation. How I wanted to learn of the experience of others in their walk with the Lord.

It only took me a couple of days to realize that little was being
said about God except in the context of right and wrong. Their
six-student school reminded me of a kennel. The worst part was
the headmistress, whose unnatural attachment for girls was em-
barrassing. Her effeminate husband was well behaved, minding
her explicit "suggestions" with such ardor that we all "knew"
that he adored her.

The staff consisted of a spinster secretary who praised the
Lord for everything from the state of her toast in the morning
to the cockroaches she found in her closet, and a single bachelor
of venerable vintage whose mind had never passed the age of
puberty.

Saintman and I were given a bedroom on the main floor of
the house. It would have been okay except that Saintman ac-
quired a dog. A rather likeable creature as a puppy, Dog grew
into a medium-sized animal of questionable intelligence. Saintman was greatly attached to him, so much so that he took him
to bed with us. His arm affectionately draped across the beast
between us, he slept undisturbed while I tried my best to keep
from touching its repulsive fur. My objections were met with
sarcasm: "You're jealous of a dog?"

Many times, I slipped out of bed and stood shivering in the
dark. What was I doing here? What in the world did all of this
have to do with God? They all talked about religion, and everyone seemed so dedicated to doing what was right. What was
wrong with me? Why did I feel so lost and alone? I felt my heart
straining for release.

Spring came with buds and fireflies. I awoke one night feeling depressed. I got up and went outside. The night stars spread
their brilliance before my startled eyes. The language of nature,
as always, seemed to argue with the circumstances of my life.

My longing for God was strong, but I was confused. What
was I really longing for? Did I not have God already?

At the commune, there was much talk about believing in
salvation because of the merits of Christ's blood, but when I
tried to get people to talk about their relationship with God, I

was counseled not to seek that which was subjective. The gospel was objective. I was reminded that it did not matter what God thought of me; it only mattered what He thought of Christ.

But, in a very tender part of my heart, it mattered a great deal what God thought of me. I couldn't have verbalized it at the time, but it really wasn't salvation that concerned me. My problem was personal identity, and what I now call "mapping." You don't build your house without a blueprint, and you can't build your life without a network of relationships.

I had so little to work from, so little understanding of people. Nearly every human contact I had experienced was distorted. I had been taught submission since birth, but not reasonableness. The only knowledge of love that I had was in my own heart, and my only joy was that bright and mostly gentle world of nature.

God's voice was always clearest to me there and so, once again, I listened outside of Scripture to learn what I could not learn from contact with people, even people who read the Bible. One night, walking in the moonlight, I prayed.

Oh God, there is something terribly wrong in this place. I hear your name all day, but it doesn't feel right. Outside, under the stars, there is no voice, but you seem so near.

Sometimes, when Saintman reads out of the Bible, I don't want to know you at all. But when I hear the wind in the trees, it feels like my heart will break with longing for you. It's almost as if there are secrets in the wind, pleasant mysteries waiting to be discovered. Will I ever know them, God?

I'm learning things all the time—what I should and shouldn't do. But I want to know you! Am I too emotional?

My mother always said I was, and so does Saintman. But I feel so much! I love the wind, the grass under my bare feet, and the sun on my hair. I hear music everywhere! When I'm outside, I feel so close to knowing you.

As before, God drew me to His heart and taught me Himself. As my eyes measured the expanse of the night sky, I felt a loosening of the bonds of narrowness that were choking my weary spirit. Going to a tree in the center of the yard, I tried to put my arms around its trunk.

How long has it taken, I wondered, for it to grow so large that my arms could not encircle it? Leaning my whole body against it, I felt its strength.

Then I realized that it was going to take me a long time to grow into understanding. Only God gives years to a tree; only God hangs stars in space. I would trust Him to grow *me*.

Going back into the house, I was relieved to see Dog stretched out on a rug. Climbing quietly back into bed with Saintman, I pondered his face. Even in sleep, severity ruled his features. Turning toward an open window, I breathed deeply of the sweet night air and let soft wind-mysteries whisper me to sleep.

Chapter Eight

Welcome, Little GirlChild

Saintman and Headmistress were on a collision course. Both were arbitrary and headstrong; it was only a matter of time before a showdown. I found it almost comical to observe them as they maneuvered around each other's offended piety.

Headmistress never let Saintman forget that she was in charge, and Saintman never let her forget that her greatest inadequacy was that she was a woman. One day he went too far. Though I never discovered exactly what happened, Saintman finally committed some infraction worthy of our dismissal. Headmistress came to me privately, put her arms around me, and tried to assuage her guilt by enlisting my sympathies. I had none to offer. I was reeling with the knowledge that we had less than fifty dollars to our name and nowhere to go.

Packing all we owned into a camper truck, Saintman, Dog, and I set off toward "home," wherever that might be. Dog panted constantly, fogging the windows and making the air foul. The back window was covered with his nose smears.

Feeling claustrophobic and full of despair, I tried to focus on something positive. As my mind searched futilely for a sweet memory or some glad dream, the movement of a grove of trees caught my eye. Rippling in turn, their collective branches seemed gracefully alive in joyous choreography. In a moment, they passed from view, but the beauty and harmony they conveyed lingered in my senses.

Two distinct worlds played against each other in my consciousness. Though I was trapped in the one, my spirit willed me to the second. If there was no harmony in my outside world, the seeds of consonance were germinating within me. It felt a great deal like I was praying. Saintman had no idea where we were headed. My course was set.

Three states away from the commune, we broke down. After repairs, we had four brown pennies left. It was time to go job hunting.

I found work first, at a dry goods store filled with colorful bolts of fabric. The different textures fascinated me, as did the button bin—a corrugated tin trough filled with buttons of all descriptions. When no one was looking, I submerged my arms in their cool smoothness, bringing up handfuls to spill in colorful rainbows of pebbly clatter back into the bin. A child's delight, I was a child peeking over the mantle of adulthood to enjoy forbidden and innocent pleasures and was satisfied.

Six months later, Mom called me at work to tell me that Nonnie had been killed. A drunken teenager had run a red light and picked her out of a crosswalk like a clay pigeon. It was the day before her eighty-fifth birthday, the day before Christmas.

A memorial service was to be held the following week. I was standing next to the cash register at the time I took the call. Customers, ready to have me cut their cloth, were watching me.

"There's really no reason for you to try to come," Mom was saying. "She won't really be there, anyway."

Her voice seemed to fade as I listened to her. She felt it served her family right that Nonnie was gone. They hadn't treated her right. She remembered the time when…

"Mom, I have to go. No, I won't try to come. I couldn't, anyway. Mom, I love you."

I was crying, trying to hide my face with my hand. As I replaced the receiver, my head rotated to the left and froze in a spasm. My employer excused me from work, and I walked to the trailer court where we parked our camper, my head still cocked painfully to one side. It took weeks of physical therapy before I could hold my head straight again. By that time I was pregnant.

Saintman told me many times that having children would interfere with his ability to serve God. He took the news of my condition sourly, but I loved the child even before my belly began to swell.

Life was cradled within me like a gentle song that needed to be sung. Though I weighed barely 110 pounds, Saintman insisted that I was fat. I saw that my upper legs were fatter than his, but he was not a large man and only slightly taller than I. Now that my body was changing, he poked fun at me when I undressed.

He also found fault with my hair. Baby-fine, it more or less went its own way. Taking a few strands between his fingers, he'd say, "Can't you *do* something?"

He wanted me to dye it Marilyn Monroe blond and even brought home a wig once and made me wear it while having sex. He called me another name and pretended that he was raping me. It frightened me and made me feel dirty.

A few months into my pregnancy, we rented a thirty-six-foot mobile home. The first thing we bought was a crib. The second was a book on natural childbirth that Saintman found. Written by a man, the book explained that it was an old wives tale that women must suffer while giving birth. Childbirth, when done properly, was painless.

That settled it for Saintman. There were to be no excuses. I was going to do it right—he would make sure of that! We enrolled in natural childbirth classes where I learned exercises and breathing techniques that ensured a joyous delivery. I tried very hard to do everything I was told. Such serious business this was, having a baby! Sometimes, though, I lay on my back and laughed at the pitch and roll of life under my bellybutton. "I love you, little baby!" I'd whisper, as if it were a secret to be kept.

During my seventh month, Saintman became extremely angered at something I did and pushed me hard, down on the bed. As I sprawled backward, he landed a kick squarely between my legs. He had hit me before, but this time more than my body hurt. Curling up into a ball, I lay very still. If God had reached down from heaven and struck my face, it couldn't have wounded me more. I had no words for my grievance.

That I should be abused was regrettable. That my unborn child should be threatened was incomprehensible. Later, as I lay awake listening to the ping of night rain on the trailer's metal roof, I tried to sort out my thoughts. In the bed next to me was the father of my unborn child. We had been married close to five years, during which time he had displayed continuous displeasure with me. I felt ugly and stupid. Why should he love me? He only tolerated me. Why should I hope for more? It was the best of love I had ever known.

A wrenching sorrow enveloped me, and my silent sobs caused the bed to jerk. Saintman stirred slightly. "Lie still!" he commanded.

My heart felt like a hydraulic lift as I endeavored to force my body to be still. While I practiced a breathing technique for labor, an enormous blackness spread over my mind.

The innocent form inside me gave a sudden, powerful kick. Instantly, my senses revived. My abdomen felt alive with movement. Two worlds, again—this time the kick of an angry man and the kick of burgeoning life. I could choose which way I faced. I placed my hand over my belly and prayed.

Oh God, the best of love I've ever known is in my own heart—for this tiny life within me! I do not know what is truth because Saintman talks about "the truth" constantly, and it is nothing I can know. I'm not sure what to think about you or why life is the way it is. But this I know: I love this child and, for now, that is all that matters.

A fierce strength trembled in my every muscle. Had I been where it was proper to do so, I would have lifted my head and roared like a mighty lioness, and the sound would have been heard across many valleys.

It seemed only a fortnight until I came full term. My body demanded that I release its energetic captive. Waking in the middle of the night, my contractions were strong—and they hurt! Panic gripped my heart.

My involuntary moaning awakened Saintman. "What's wrong?" he asked.

"I think I'm in labor," I replied. My heart was beating wildly, but I didn't dare let him know how much it hurt.

"Well, start breathing properly!" he commanded. But no amount of breathing relieved the terrible pain. It just kept getting worse, and Saintman kept getting angrier. "You're not doing it right!"

"I'm trying! Please, I'm trying!" I cried between breaths.

"No you're not!" he said severely. "If you were, it wouldn't hurt!"

Finally he called the doctor. When the doctor asked to speak to me, Saintman said, "She's losing her head. You'd better tell her to get hold of herself!"

The doctor's voice was gentle. "How are you doing, Honey?"

"It hurts!" I cried. "No matter what I do, it hurts!"

There was a small silence. "Of course it hurts," he said soothingly. "You're having a baby. Don't be afraid. Come on in to the hospital, and we'll take care of you."

"He said it would hurt," I explained to Saintman as we made our way to the emergency room.

"Sure," he retorted. "What does *he* know? But *you* know better. You're without excuse!"

Miserable inside and out, I was installed in the labor room. Saintman asked to stay with me to help me breathe correctly. The pain made me beyond caring. When the doctor came to examine me, he sent Saintman out of the room. A little while later he came around to my side and took my hand.

"We have a little problem here," he said gently. "You're doing great, but you're going to need a little help. Don't be frightened. Your baby is doing fine. We're going to take you into the delivery room now."

"Please don't let my husband in again," I pleaded.

"Don't you worry, Sweetheart!" blurted an attending nurse. "He won't get within a hundred feet of you. I'll make sure of that!" She was built like a marine, and I had little doubt she'd keep her promise.

The next few minutes were all confusion. I was placed on a gurney and rolled down a hall to a very bright room. Suddenly, someone covered my nose and mouth with a rubber cup. I couldn't breathe and struggled to escape. No one had warned me that this would happen. I went wild with panic.

Then the room started to swing and turn. It seemed like I was miles away from my body.

God, Help me! I can't breathe. Where are you? My baby…

Then I was waking up. The room was hushed. I didn't hurt anymore. The doctor spoke soothingly.

"We're just about finished. You did great, Honey. You had a block, but we fixed that up just fine. You have a little girl!"

I propped up on an elbow. There on a gurney next to me was a tiny bit of pink flesh wrapped in a soft white blanket.

"Aren't you going to touch her?" the doctor asked.

Was she *mine*? I reached out and touched her with one finger, then quickly withdrew it. I felt nothing! Shame flooded my heart—what was wrong with me? I was shaking all over.

The nurse brought a warm blanket and tucked it in all around me. As the shaking subsided, I turned again to my little baby girl-child. Suddenly a thought struck me.

Oh my God! No one's holding her! She's so little—precious little GirlChild, I love you. I love you so very much!

Then the nurse was taking her away. "I want to hold her!" I cried. "Wait! Let me *hold* her!"

But the nurse, very much in charge, marched away with my baby. Forcing myself to be calm, I tried to push away the feeling of resentment that overwhelmed me. I would not cry. Most of all, I would not let little GirlChild ever experience what I had known since my birth. She would know that she mattered. She would know love.

When they finally brought her back to me, I held her over my heart and whispered, "Welcome, Little One. Do you hear me? I said that you are *welcome!*

Chapter Nine

Solitaire

The sun shinning through the window threw shadow stripes into GirlChild's crib, but it was bitterly cold outside. It had been snowing for days. The wind had piled up huge drifts of the stuff. All traffic in the streets had stopped, and sound was muffled like the world was wrapped in bunting.

Saintman sat at the kitchen table playing solitaire. Game after game, hour after hour, he stayed locked in his private world. We were poor and I had read everything in the house three times over. We didn't own a television or even a radio. We didn't have a phone, either, but it would have made little difference. Our social life consisted of Saintman's Bible studies.

Twice a week GirlChild and I accompanied him to people's homes where he conducted meetings. If I ever ventured a word or an opinion, he either ignored me, or, if he was sufficiently aggravated, closed his Bible with a thud and announced that it was time for us to leave. On the way home he lectured me about the inappropriateness of my interruption.

He was playing life solitaire.

GirlChild was nearing her seventh month. Tiny for her age, she was almost lost in her blankets as she slept. Saintman had read somewhere that children should not be given what they cry for and got it into his head that she should be taught patience. I tried to explain that what applies to children may not apply to little babies. Before they can talk, crying is the only way a baby can communicate. He wouldn't listen.

One day it was time for GirlChild's next feeding. I had to be quicker this time. I couldn't let her cry!

"Fix me some orange juice." Saintman didn't bother to look at me as he spoke. I hesitated, glancing quickly at GirlChild. She had just begun to stir. Saintman looked up at me.

"Hurry up," he said impatiently.

"GirlChild is waking up…" I began.

"She can wait. It won't take you very long." His eyes were hard.

I hurried to the kitchen, noting that GirlChild was beginning her little "I'm awake" whimpers. My hands didn't move fast enough; I spilled the juice when I poured it into a glass. GirlChild was now fully awake, and her voice was taking on real volume.

Setting the glass before Saintman, I rushed toward the crib. GirlChild had crawled to one end and was pulling herself upright, crying lustily. As I reached for her, I noticed how wet she was. Quickly offering her my breast, I headed for the back bedroom to change her.

Before I could squeeze by Saintman, he pushed his chair back and blocked the doorway, his eyebrows raised in that angry arch I so feared. His mouth was set.

"My mother cured my little sister of tantrums," he declared as he jerked her out of my arms, "by putting her in a tub of cold water."

The abruptness of his action caused GirlChild to wail with new intensity, and her face turned red from the strain. I tried to get her back into my arms, but Saintman was determined. He headed for the bathroom.

"She's only seven months old," I protested. "Your sister was almost ten!"

The bathroom was so small I couldn't reach around him. He turned on the tap.

"If my mom had started earlier, she wouldn't have had the problem in the first place!"

Saintman's voice was deathly calm. I began beating him on the back, begging him to stop. GirlChild was hysterical. Her feet and arms churned wildly. Saintman tightened his hold on her. I felt as though I had a geyser inside of me rising to spew a hundred feet into the air. Panic and helplessness blew through my senses, and I fled. I couldn't stop him. I couldn't protect GirlChild!

"Help! Somebody help me!" I screamed as I ran out into the snow. "My baby!"

But the snow muffled my voice against my face. I ran until I fell into a large drift. Snow filled my mouth and eyes, but I still felt the heat of my tears. I lay still, letting the cold numb me. My spirit was broken.

How could you? She is so little—or have you deserted me?

God seemed so far away—invisible, as though I were standing, face pressed against a glass that was covered with smoke, trying to see God on the other side.

I don't know what I expected to hear in answer from God, but hearing nothing, a thought struck me.

Saintman claims you. Well, you can have him. And if he is yours, then I cannot be. I cannot stand it any longer. I cannot pretend it's okay. I know I'm going against your will, but if I have to stay with Saintman in order to obey you, then I will have to leave both of you.

How long was I in the snow? I don't remember. When I returned to the trailer, there was no feeling left in me. I was not hungry or cold or angry. Life seemed two-dimensional—like a picture in a book, as though I could see and hear everything but was no longer a part of what was happening.

No sound came from inside the trailer. When I opened the door Saintman was seated at the kitchen table, his Bible in front of him. Turning toward me, he spoke with disgust.

"Some mother you are! Your baby is hungry."

Moving to the crib, I looked down at little GirlChild. She was wrapped in a towel, lying very still, eyes wide open. She made no sound as I picked her up.

"See?" Saintman said.

In the back bedroom I put GirlChild's cold little mouth to my empty breast. She suckled briefly, her eyes still opened wide. I knew what had to be done.

"I can't be your mommy anymore," I told her softly as I diapered and dressed her. "I can't protect you. I can't even feed you. And I can't take you with me, because I am leaving God and I don't want you to go to hell with me. Someday you'll understand."

GirlChild was totally subdued. I studied her face. She was so beautiful! Her eyes closed slowly, and she slept. Returning her to her crib, I went back to the bedroom and took down the one suitcase we owned. It was easy to pack. I didn't have that much to take.

Saintman was playing solitaire when I set my bag down in the kitchen. He seemed to understand what I was doing. Without looking at me he spoke.

"So you really *are* that kind of woman. I figured as much."

Yes, I guess I am, I thought. No decent mother would leave her baby. But I'm leaving *God*. I'm going to hell. I can't take her with me. I have to go alone.

Saintman laid three twenty-dollar bills on the table. Where did he get that kind of money! I picked the bills up, walked out, and made my way to a bus station. I was shaking violently from the cold and from what I'd just done. The ticket agent could barely understand me. I told him that I wanted to go south. Where? I didn't know. What did he suggest? Picking one of the cities he named, I paid my fare. The bus was outside and ready to leave.

Only two other people got on, taking back seats. I chose a front seat because I always got carsick. We headed out in a swinging lurch. The driver, an oily, meaty-looking man, turned and smiled at me.

"Where y'headed?" he asked.

"South." I looked away.

"Visiting relatives?" His face was reflected imperfectly in a large, battered mirror that hung at an angle in the front of the bus.

"No."

The seats were soiled, the ashtrays on their arms stuffed with gum wrappers. Bus Driver said something else, but I didn't answer. Exhausted, I fell asleep against the window. I woke up feeling startled and disoriented just as the bus door whooshed open.

We had traveled some distance toward our destination while I slept. Bus Driver got off and helped the other passengers step down. When I didn't get off, he got back on and sat down in the seat next to me.

"Alone, huh?" he grinned. "Want somethin' to eat?"

I didn't like the way he spoke. He was too friendly.

"No thanks."

He sat there grinning, looking at me. When I blushed, he leaned toward me.

"Hey, I know a really nice place up the line. We could go and get warm."

I knew I was going to hell, but I also knew that I'd get there on my own terms!

"I don't think my husband would approve," I said, not caring at all whether Saintman approved.

"How's he ever gonna know?"

Bus Driver leaned even closer. Drops of saliva oozed between his lips and formed beads in the corners of his mouth.

" 'Cause I'm gonna tell him!" I said angrily.

Bus Driver pulled back, muttered some words under his breath that I did not understand, and got up, giving the seat a sharp slap. He got back off the bus and walked toward a small diner. Watching him, I saw a car drive straight toward him. It was going to hit him! Then, as if in a dream, it appeared to pass right through him.

My heart was pounding as I leaned back in my seat. I had been watching a double reflection caused by my window and the glass in the open bus door! Without even thinking, I prayed.

Life is like that. It's all so confusing—like a double reflection. How can I tell if things are real or not? Maybe even you aren't real. Maybe I've been seeing a spiritual double reflection. I'm so tired, so very tired. There's just nothing left in me, God. I don't even feel up to hell!

It was late afternoon when we reached a large city. Getting off the bus, I walked toward some tall buildings. Realizing that I was in a very seedy part of town, but not knowing what else to do, I just kept walking. Four tough-looking young men came toward me, their eyes fixed on mine. My blood went cold.

I couldn't run, so I looked straight ahead and kept going. I got to within inches of them before they parted, hooting and making unseemly remarks. I walked right through them, just like Bus Driver walked through the car. My mind seemed to be groping for something congruent. How tired I felt!

Reaching the main downtown section, I thought, *I have to get a job.* As if anyone got a job, transportation, and a place to stay all at a quarter to five in the afternoon! I turned in at an office of some sort and asked a receptionist, "Are you hiring anyone?"

She just stared at me. Finally, she looked down and answered very softly, "No."

Going back outside, I was beginning to get frightened. It would be dark in less than an hour, and I had nowhere to go. I couldn't even pray—I'd left God.

Glancing sideways I happened to catch sight of myself in a large window, and what I saw made me jerk to a stop. I looked like I'd been tangling with a gorilla! But I had no time to lose, so I went in at the next building—a bank.

Going up to a desk, I spoke matter-of-factly: "Are you looking for any help?"

The girl recoiled. She started to send me away when a voice from the back called out, "Stop! Come here, I want to talk to you."

A nice-looking gentleman started toward me. Suddenly, I felt humiliated. Frozen, I put my head down.

He touched my sleeve gently. "Come and sit down."

Drawing me toward his desk, he began talking to me. He asked if I needed help. Without looking up, I told him I needed a job.

He was quiet for a moment. Okay, he'd get me a job. Did I have a place to stay?

I must have given him the same look I'd given Bus Driver, because he immediately started talking about his wife. Then he made a phone call. After a minute of conversation, he put the phone down and said he would take me for an interview to a place where he was sure I would get work, but he wanted to stop first at a florist's shop and get his wife some flowers.

It was Valentine's Day.

Chapter Ten

He Knew My Hurt

Kind Man must have understood how vulnerable I was. And how hungry. I suddenly realized that I hadn't eaten in several days. No wonder I had had no milk for GirlChild! Handing me some money, he told me to run around the corner and buy a sandwich.

"Make sure you come back!" he called after me as I left the building.

I bought the sandwich and took a bite. It stuck in my throat. When I got back to the bank the door was locked. As I turned to go, someone opened the door and motioned me in. Kind Man waved me to his desk where he was stuffing papers into a leather briefcase. Then we were off to my interview with the personnel director of the largest savings and loan company in the city.

On the way there he briefed me. They were always in need of tellers. Could I add and subtract easily? I told him I could. He said I should be sure to say that positively to the woman who would interview me. Her name reminded me of a tossed salad. He said that Mrs. Salad was a generous professional who would make sure I was all right.

"You're going to be Okay, Kid," he reassured me. "She'll take care of you!"

He dropped me off at the front door and was gone. Following his instructions, I took the elevator to the top floor. The doors opened into a lovely room with live trees growing in huge pots.

"Hi! Are you the girl coming for an interview? Mrs. Salad is waiting for you."

The slender, bright-eyed receptionist who greeted me didn't look any older than my twenty-four years. Leading me into a spacious, well-furnished office, Bright Eyes presented me to Mrs. Salad, who looked every bit as gracious as Kind Man had said she was. Her silvered hair was set softly and skillfully around her expressive face. She invited me to sit down on a blue-velvet sofa.

"Tell me about yourself," she began.

I was so tired. More than anything else, I wanted to curl up on the couch in her softly lit office and forget everything.

"There's nothing to tell," I replied blankly. Then I started to cry.

Cruelty I was prepared for. Kindness left me undone. I felt ashamed. She wanted to help me, and I couldn't even help her to help me.

"Can you add? Are you willing to learn how to handle a bank window?" she said, watching me carefully.

"I'll give it all I've got," I answered truthfully.

She stood up and walked around her desk. Sitting down beside me on the couch, she touched my arm.

"You look like a battered child, but something tells me that it will be worth the effort to help you. Do you have a place to stay tonight? No, of course you don't." She answered the question herself.

I was sent home with Bright Eyes. In the morning I would begin the process of being hired. For a fleeting moment I thought to myself, *God is watching over me!* Then I remembered: He couldn't be. I had left Him. An awful hollow feeling engulfed me. I was so used to praying. Now I couldn't anymore.

Bright Eyes lived on the outskirts of town with two other girls. A jovial bunch, they clucked and chattered and made me take a bath. Then they made me eat. One of them offered me some liquor.

"I don't drink," I said without thinking.

"Well, Honey, you'd better start!" one of the girls answered. "You're going to need help facing cold reality." She handed me a glass of foul smelling fluid.

I took one swallow and nearly threw up. It tasted like an old drain pipe smells and felt hot all the way down. The girls howled. Bright Eyes had an idea. "Hey! Let's give her a screwdriver!"

I couldn't imagine what they meant and was totally baffled when they gave me a glass of orange juice. *That* I could handle, though it tasted a little sour. In a few minutes I felt like I was floating. Then I went to bed. I don't remember hitting the sheets.

The next morning I awoke to the scurry of bed making, breakfast grabbing, and the blare of the local radio station. Looking into my suitcase, I was at a loss as to what to wear. All I had was one dress, one skirt, and an assortment of mismatched pants and tops. Choosing the dress, I presented myself to the girls.

"Good morning!" the girls said. "How do you feel? Did you guess? We put vodka in your juice—and almost had to carry you to bed!"

So that was it. I smiled sheepishly.

"We'd better watch out for this little chickie," one of the girls said affectionately. "She doesn't know the time of day!"

"Speaking of the time of day," Bright Eyes interrupted, "we're going to be late. Let's go!"

With that, we raced out the door and into my new life. For the next few days I was photographed, fingerprinted, bonded, and probed. At last I was pronounced "ready." Except that I was not.

My stay with Bright Eyes and her roommates was fast turning into a nightmare. At first I had no hint. Then Bright Eyes' friend showed up. A large girl with close-cropped hair, she marched in like some sort of football hero. That evening, as she cuddled and stroked Bright Eyes, I knew I needed to be thinking of some other living arrangement. The other roommates cuddled each other.

Mrs. Salad must have suspected something all along. She kept asking me if things were working out at Bright Eyes'. Finally she asked me point blank about Bright Eyes' "orientation." When I told her that I didn't want to live there, she sighed.

"Well, you'll just have to live with me. I was going to suggest that in the first place, but thought you'd rather be with girls your own age."

"You don't have to do that," I protested. But she would have none of it.

"Nonsense! Since my daughter got married, the house has been altogether too quiet."

I went home with her that night, after we stopped by a shopping center to buy me "a few things." Several dresses, shoes, and a shampoo later, we went home. The next day, I was on the teller line.

Mrs. Salad's husband welcomed me as graciously as she had. Like Bright Eyes' roommates, though, he decided I needed to learn how to drink.

"We'll start tonight!" he declared one evening after work.

We dressed and went to dinner at their favorite restaurant. Deciding to alleviate their fears, when the waiter asked me what I wanted to drink, I announced that I'd have a screwball.

"A *what?*" the waiter asked in amazement.

Mrs. Salad's husband roared with laughter and nearly fell off his chair.

"She...she wants...she wants a...*screwball!*

Even Mrs. Salad could not contain herself. Dabbing her eyes, she tried to gain her composure. I was mortified.

"You know," I said, wishing I could die. "It's what Bright Eyes and her roommates gave me. Orange juice with, uh..."

After that Mrs. Salad's husband redoubled his efforts to educate me in the ways of the world. Fixing me a scotch or bourbon every night, he encouraged me to learn how to drink. I couldn't stand the stuff and dumped it into a certain potted plant when he wasn't looking. It developed "halitosis," but I was complimented on how well I held my liquor.

I had been gone from GirlChild one month. One night I

awoke, intensely alive with her memory. In a mighty convulsion, I lunged from my bed and out into the hall, unable to catch my breath.

"My baby! My baby! I've got to get my baby!"

Life had come full cycle. Compelled beyond my own deliberateness, I could now only follow the reawakened instincts of my shattered motherhood. Whatever it meant, I had to be with GirlChild again.

Mrs. Salad immediately took charge. Though she was shocked to learn that I had a baby, she was horrified that I had not even seen a lawyer, and engaged her own attorney that very night. Divorce proceedings were begun the next day as plans were made for the retrieval of my baby. A plane ticket was purchased. I was to fly to where she was, snatch her and run. There was just one catch: I needed someone on that end to help me. Mrs. Salad asked if I knew anyone there I could trust.

At first I said I didn't. Then I remembered a doctor who had treated me when Nonnie died. He had seemed concerned about my situation with Saintman. Putting in a call to him, I was amazed at how quickly he agreed to help.

"Don't worry, Little One. You've been through enough. I'll be there," he told me over the phone.

No one had ever called me "Little One" before. Something deep inside of me stirred, but there were no words for it—just a tiny spot of warmth.

So it was set. Doctor would meet my plane and take me to GirlChild's baby sitter. How he knew where she was, I never learned. I was stunned by his compassion. Almost twenty years my senior, he had never married. Perhaps he felt fatherly toward me. Every conversation was peppered with his endearments. It was hard to keep from crying when I heard his voice.

All went according to plan. Though I got airsick, I arrived without mishap. Doctor was there, quickly taking me in his arms and telling me that everything was going to be Okay. I wanted so much to believe him.

We went directly to the baby sitter's. A woman from our church answered the door. Though she was surprised to see me, she didn't try to stop me from going to where GirlChild was sleeping. When I leaned over and picked her up, she opened her eyes. Instantly, she began to "talk" excitedly, smiling and waving her arms about. I kissed her face all over and headed for the door. The baby sitter offered no interference.

The next few hours have become a jumble in my memory. My thoughts, my arms, were full of GirlChild. That's all I know. Mrs. Salad was ready for our arrival. She had purchased a lovely playpen with a luxuriously thick mat. Her cupboards were bursting with jars of baby food, and a bottle of warm milk waited on the stove. I was exhausted.

The next couple of weeks were filled with consultations with Mrs. Salad's lawyer, angry messages from Saintman and many happy hours with GirlChild. Things settled into a pattern of work and motherhood. As the days passed, however, I realized that I needed to get a place of my own.

My bedroom at Mrs. Salad's belonged to her married daughter, and all her things were still there. Though grateful for a place to stay, it wasn't "home." And, though Mrs. Salad genuinely enjoyed GirlChild's presence, I was increasingly aware of my baby's innocent exploration of objects far too accessible and far too valuable.

Mrs. Salad insisted that I locate in a huge apartment complex not far from her home.

"You've got to be around people," she advised. "You don't know what Saintman will try."

Consequently, I moved into a very nice flat, cavernously empty save for one chair and a lamp in the front room, and a Hollywood bed and crib in the bedroom. Mrs. Salad purchased a high chair, giving the kitchen one bright corner. She also paid to have a phone installed.

That first night, alone, with no TV or radio to break the silence, I lay in the darkness listening to GirlChild's soft, nighttime mumblings. Again and again my heart lurched toward God, only to stop short, knowing the sin I thought I had committed. And when I cried, I did not call His name.

Feeling abandoned by God as I had abandoned Him, my soul grieved with helpless shame. In place of God's "voice" in my heart, I heard only Saintman's harsh condemnation. Then, as if someone had taken the needle from a record, I heard nothing at all.

A strange quiet pressed against my heart, like when sleep overtakes a blistering fever. I had no capacity to comprehend it at the time, but I now know that God took this poor child into His great arms. Wordlessly, He shut me in with Him, for He knew my hurt, and I rested.

Chapter Eleven

Kidnapped!

"Mrs. Salad, GirlChild took her first steps today at the baby sitter's!"

I was so excited, I was yelling into the phone.

"I missed it, but tonight she walked for me too."

In a few minutes, Mrs. Salad arrived to see the wondrous feat for herself. She had with her an envelope. In a little while she opened it and took out a wedding ring.

Handing it to me, she explained, "This was my mother's wedding ring. I want you to wear it on the teller line. It will help to protect you."

Taking the delicate ring, I slipped it onto my finger. Though I had said nothing to anyone, I had been feeling vexed at the flirtatious advances of certain male customers. It seemed that the more money they had, the brasher they were, verbally.

Mrs. Salad's voice interrupted my thoughts. She told me that my supervisor was going to have a baby.

"I want you to consider training into her position. I know you are under a lot of pressure, but I really think you can handle it. You learn fast and are dependable. It will be a step toward even greater responsibility."

I didn't answer her immediately. My mind could hardly grasp the idea that I might be capable of such advancement. I was still so transparent to myself. It was true that I enjoyed learning—I always had. But for someone to place confidence in me was a new experience.

From somewhere inside me a voice arose, so familiar, so painful that it startled me. "If you try, they'll find out! Somehow, you've fooled them into thinking you're all right. You know you're not."

I'd heard the voice all my life. At first it was hazy, like the slow rising of dust when you ride a bike fast over a dirt driveway. As I grew older, it took on more definition and passed itself as self-honesty. Yet even then I sensed its variance. It was like it really didn't come from my own conscience. When I married Saintman I didn't hear it any more. I didn't have to. He said it all.

"I'll think about it," I told Mrs. Salad. "And thank you for the ring. I'll take good care of it."

"I know you will," she responded, smiling. "It's very valuable, but especially so to me. I'm glad it fits you."

I looked down at the precious gold encircling my finger. *Mrs. Salad's mother must have been a worthy person*, I thought. Her ring seemed a testimony of value beyond a jeweler's carat. I felt myself being nudged toward an understanding of my own worth and of a potential within myself that I had never known before—or hadn't dared allow myself to know.

I had felt this way on occasion. The feeling was like a tiny flame struggling to take hold on the wick of a candle. Always before I'd blown it out. Maybe, if I were given a chance, Mrs. Salad's appraisal of me would prove accurate. This time I didn't blow out the flickering flame. I let it burn, and enjoyed its warmth.

A little while after Mrs. Salad left, the phone rang. It was Doctor. He had been calling every day. Though I appreciated hearing from him at first, I was growing a little edgy, like I was being led down a narrow hallway. I tried to convince myself that everything was all right, that I should be grateful to have such a considerate and concerned friend.

Doctor told me that he was coming down on a business trip and wanted to see me. He had a present for GirlChild. Pushing aside my feelings of entrapment, I spoke the expected words of gladness, hung up, grabbed GirlChild, and headed outside.

The sun was making puzzle-piece shadows all over the patio to the accompaniment of wildly happy bird songs. I felt my heart throbbing as tears spilled from my eyes. If only I could have GirlChild and God at the same time! Inside my mouth my tongue took the shape of His name, but I did not speak it, even in my mind.

Doctor visited several times in the next few weeks, bringing food and presents for GirlChild. We often went riding in his car. One afternoon we stopped at a park. While we were walking, he asked me to marry him, but told me that I needed to know something before giving him my answer. Taking my hand, he explained why he'd never married before. He was homosexual.

"We make better husbands," he said with a smile. "We're loyal and sensitive and…"

I felt like I was caught on a huge swing, coming down from a terrible height, backward, sickeningly backward. My eyes clawed at the earth, though not a grass blade moved. How could life be like this? Suddenly, I felt very tired.

"Please, take me home." My words felt flat as they came from my mouth. "I need to get home."

Doctor nodded. "I know you'll be able to handle this," he said. 'You are a special person."

GirlChild was asleep in my arms when we reached my apartment. Doctor got out, came around to my side of the car, and opened the door. He started to follow me to the building, but I turned to face him.

"No," I said quietly.

He hesitated, eyebrows raised slightly.

I lowered my head and repeated the word. "No."

He stood there for a long moment.

"Thank you for everything," I said softly. "I'm sorry."

A look of dignity flashed in his eyes. Taking a deep breath he said, "Goodbye. Goodbye, Little One."

I turned and walked to my door. I heard him drive away as I went inside.

I put GirlChild in her crib, came back to the front room, and lay across the rug. At first I did not cry. I was tired of crying. But then it came, like a thaw when streams overflow their banks in a rush to the sea. Sorrow shook my whole body, sorrow for Doctor, for myself, for the whole world.

I didn't want to hurt him, but you can't catch water in cheesecloth. I was so confused. He had seemed more like a father than a suitor to me. Or did he? What was a father supposed to be like, anyway? Memories from childhood pushed toward my consciousness, only to fall back into darkness. Fearing that I was mentally ill, I sat up and drew my knees to my chest, forcing myself to be calm. I spoke out loud.

"I am sitting here on this rug crying because someone who shouldn't have asked me to marry him did. I am crying because I'm lonely, because I don't have a father or a mother."

I got up and walked into the bedroom and looked at GirlChild, damp with sleep. I had no answers and there was a stone of agony in my guts, but I knew one thing for certain: I loved GirlChild. Going to my bed, I lay down with my eyes fixed on my sleeping baby until I, too, fell asleep.

Not long after that, Saintman was granted visitation privileges. Given GirlChild's age, the court stipulated that his time with her should be in my presence. Though this terrified me, I was glad for GirlChild's sake. Instinctively, I did not trust him alone with her.

And so it began. Saintman, pious with an air of damaged rights, came each Sunday to see his daughter. He insisted on taking her out to the patio, alone, or into the next room. It made me uneasy because he never made a sound while he had her out of my sight. There was deliberateness about his actions that frightened me.

One Sunday afternoon, Saintman turned to me with tears in his eyes. He said that he'd noticed how empty my cupboards were, and offered to take me to the store to buy groceries. I was surprised. He usually said any trouble I had proved that God had forsaken me.

At first I declined, but relented when he said that it wasn't fair of me to deny GirlChild provisions that he was willing to give. That it was utterly selfish of me to hold a grudge against him that would bring hardship on our baby.

There was a supermarket just across the street from the apartment complex. When we entered the store, Saintman placed GirlChild in a shopping cart. He motioned for me to take a second cart and told me to get whatever I needed. He would pay for it. When I objected to separate carts, he became angry.

"For crying out loud," he spoke at full volume. "Here I am buying you groceries and you still have to act this way! I just want to show GirlChild around. You're a mental case!"

Seeing me cringe, he started down an aisle.

"I'll stay within calling distance," he said coldly.

I pushed my cart down the aisle after him, trying to pull myself together. I felt ridiculous. He was right. I was acting stupidly. Looking at boxes and cans, I made an effort to choose what I thought I needed.

Before long, Saintman had turned a corner. Hurrying to catch up, I entered the aisle just as he was about to turn another corner. Glancing at me, he threw me an "oh brother" look and disappeared. After several such occurrences, with the distance between us lengthening, it finally happened. When I turned the corner, he wasn't there.

My heart was racing, but I forced myself to pick out a couple of items before turning down the next aisle. Again pacing myself, I pushed the cart blindly down to and around the corner. No sign of GirlChild and Saintman.

Panic seized my heart, and I raced down the next aisle and the next, finally leaving my cart entirely to run the length of the store. Looking down every aisle, my knees began to buckle as I went from one checkout stand to another, asking if anyone had seen a man with a baby leave the store. My voice was shaking so badly that I'm not sure anyone really understood what I was saying.

With no positive answer, I ran home on legs that seemed partially paralyzed.

"Saintman, Saintman, where are you?" I cried as I ran.

Of course, there was no answer. The apartment was empty, as I knew it would be. Heading back to the supermarket, I tried to spot his car. He never parked where I could see it, so I had no idea where to look. After checking the store, it was apparent that Saintman was gone.

I moved heavily as I made my way back home, feeling as if I were under a hundred pounds of water. When I got into the house, I dialed the operator and asked for the police. A moment later, a nasal voice came on the line.

"My baby!" I screamed. "My baby's been kidnapped!"

A female voice asked for my name, then my address.

"When did the kidnapping occur?"

I went wild. "He's taken my baby! Please help me!"

"Who's taken your baby, Ma'am?" she intoned.

"My husband. I mean my ex-husband. Well, almost ex. I mean…"

When she told me that the police did not interfere with domestic squabbles, I slumped to the floor and let go of the receiver. It was hopeless, anyway. Saintman had taken GirlChild, and God was with him.

I hung up and called Mrs. Salad. She came immediately, took the phone and called her lawyer. Soon an officer appeared and took down all the information I could give him. Though sympathetic, he was blunt. Saintman was the child's natural father. There was little the police could do. Mrs. Salad made an indistinguishable noise in her throat. When he left, she called her attorney back.

"Don't panic," he assured her. "These guys usually get tired of a baby in a matter of hours. At best, he'll keep her a few days. At any rate, he can't be that smart. We'll get him!"

I was not comforted. As the next days passed, I obediently did what everyone told me to do. Then a letter arrived from Saintman stating that he was taking GirlChild behind the iron curtain. He said he knew God was with him because he had succeeded in getting her away from me. I would never see my baby again. God had forsaken me completely.

I believed every word of it—almost. In the hours of exhaustion and grief since GirlChild had been kidnapped, I finally fell openly into God's arms and knew instantly that He had been there all along, waiting for me. With the knowing, like the clearest sounding of a bell, it came to me what I needed to do.

I called a certain man, a believer, whom I knew Saintman greatly admired, explained what had happened, and asked for help. He was very kind and offered to try to help me contact Saintman. The next day he called back.

"I know where he is," he said.

Chapter Twelve

I Have a Father!

Saintman was hiding with some believers several states away. I was not told who they were, only that GirlChild was all right. If I dropped divorce proceedings, Saintman would consent to be reunited with me. It had to be in writing.

My attorney was furious when I told him to drop proceedings.

"That's exactly what he expected you to do!" he yelled. "Stick to your guns! We'll nail his hide to the wall!"

He didn't know that I'd made a promise to God. In my mind, going back to God meant going back to Saintman. That there might have been other options—that I might have been able to retrieve GirlChild without having to place myself in a perilous relationship with a man who was potentially criminal, was beyond my capacity to understand.

Mrs. Salad tried to talk me out of my decision. She feared for my safety. However, since the words she spoke were not in a religious context, I rejected them. The church had taught me to believe that reasonableness was valid only, as it were, in choir robes. I took off her mother's wedding ring and handed it back to her.

She sighed deeply as she slowly closed her hand over the delicate gold band. Too professional to be given to emotional demonstration, she sat in silence, head down, as if studying the weave of her linen skirt. Then she rose and left me alone in my empty apartment. I never saw her again.

After placing a call to The Believers, I went into the bedroom to pack. Getting down the old suitcase, I once again gathered my belongings, leaving the pretty things Mrs. Salad had purchased for me on my bed.

GirlChild's things fit into two shopping bags. Not daring to glance at the pretty high chair in the kitchen, I walked out of the apartment for the last time. In a few minutes I was picked up and taken to a bus station, where I purchased a ticket that would take me halfway across the United States. The Believers knew of Saintman's whereabouts and offered to take me in temporarily.

Two days later I arrived, worn to the bone, and was taken to an old farmhouse where The Believers lived. I was accepted as a repenting sinner, a woman of disrepute "come home." They treated me kindly, thanking God that I had finally submitted to His will. I settled down to wait. Saintman had disappeared again, telling no one of his whereabouts.

One night after everybody was asleep, I crept down an old staircase and out onto a sagging porch where thorny rosebushes wound their tendrils up toward the roof. A long-abandoned wicker chair dominated one corner, its broken cushion offering comfort to a huge cat with eyes the color of sea foam. My heart was so heavy it seemed to be hanging in my stomach as I sat down on the top step. I needed to pray out loud, so I covered my mouth with my hand.

Well, God, here I am. It's what you wanted. I've come back to you.

For a minute, all I could do was cry. I felt so defeated. But I was with God again, and for that I could not feel bad.

I wanted you all along. I'm so sorry! I'll never leave you again. If I have to die, I will die in your presence. If I have to crawl, I'll crawl to you. If I have to be ignorant all of my life, I will bury my ignorant face in your arms and let my shame be hidden in your holy robes. *I don't know how I am going to live, but I will live every day knowing that I belong to you.*

Stepping down off the porch, I wandered toward the pasture. I looked up into the sky and wished I could see into heaven, but instead I seemed to be looking through smoked glass.

Oh God, how can it be that a man like Saintman finds favor with you? He is so cruel. Sometimes I wonder if he knows you at all. I am so confused!

A deep-voiced cow nearby interrupted my thoughts. I could barely make out her bulky form. Blandly content, she stood under the same canopy of night that I did, both of us captives of creation. A mouthful of re-chewed grass was all she desired. My serenity would not come so easily. Again I prayed.

So many times I wanted to cry out to you, but couldn't. Did you know? I needed you so badly!

Suddenly, and with startling clarity, the story of the demoniac who had rushed to Jesus in the synagogue, cursing and swearing, came to my mind. Though the poor man could utter only vile oaths, Jesus understood the cry of his poor, captive heart and delivered him.

A new understanding flooded my mind.

You knew all along! You knew how desperately I needed you— that I never really wanted to leave you!

Reverence for God engulfed my whole being. I spoke slowly now, softly.

You never left me. You kept your hand over me the whole time!

I stood silently in the darkness for a long time. The darkness that had engulfed me all my life had begun to be overturned!

Though I could not possibly sort through all that had happened or understand the circumstances that were still mine, a new thought was born in my mind. With great wonder, I let my voice wrap around it.

You protected me, even when I ran away from you. You loved me enough to see past my actions and into my heart. You accepted me the whole time. You...are my Father. You are my FATHER. I have a Father!

I was laughing now, the happy laughter of jubilee. Running back toward the yard I kicked off my shoes and began to dance barefooted in the wet grass. FATHER—the cursed word had become a harvest in the midst of my impoverishment. My feelings were childlike, exploring, and exuberant. It was the first time that I liked the idea that God was my Father.

I do not know how long I danced. Winded, I sat down again on the porch. Though I was very happy, GirlChild's absence weighed upon my heart. Would Saintman bring her back to me? Surely it was God's will that such a little child be with her mother.

Saintman talked a lot about obeying God and doing His will, but then did things that were ugly and hurtful. He told me that it was God's will that a wife submit to her husband and he read passages in the Scriptures to prove it. Church teaching seemed to validate him. Using that as a basis for his authority over me, he ordered me around like an ill-trained animal and punished me when dissatisfied with my performance.

He talked about self-denial and made me fast, chastising me when it made me sick. It was the will of God, he said, that I be healthy. My weakness was evidence that I was in some way out of harmony with God's plan.

As I sat thinking about these things, I knew I wanted to obey God's will, but was it always God's will for me to do what Saintman said? How was I to know for sure?

Oh my Father, I prayed, aware of His name on my tongue. *Teach me your will.*

I knew of nothing in me that was resistant to this God who was my Father. He had not forsaken me in my sin. I could trust Him with my life.

And though I know I don't deserve it, please bring my baby back to me. I love her so much! I want to take care of her. I don't want her to ever go through what I have experienced. Please, Father, for her sake!

A few days later Saintman called The Believers. They assured him that my repentance was genuine. The divorce proceedings had been dropped. He agreed to return.

A week later I was given instructions to meet him at a train station about fifty miles north of the farm. I was to go alone. Borrowing The Believer's car, I made the journey.

The day was bright. My heart sent tremors down to my toes as I parked outside the station and walked in, feeling like I had the flu. Soon I was standing on the platform, straining my eyes down the tracks for a train.

In the distance a whistle blew. A few moments later a locomotive appeared. With a roar, the train slowed to a stop and spewed cargo and passengers onto the dock. Saintman and GirlChild were not among them.

Soon other passengers began to board. I sat down on a nearby bench and began to cry. Had he changed his mind? Would I never see my baby again? Not knowing what else to do, I just sat there watching the train move on down the line.

After a while, another train pulled in. There, in one of the windows, I spotted Saintman. He was not smiling, but I jumped up and down and waved. When he got up I could see GirlChild. I lost track of his movements inside the train, so moved to where everyone was disembarking and waited.

It seemed forever before he was in the doorway, then descending. GirlChild was poorly clad and rumpled, but looked more precious than I had ever seen her. When she saw me, she started babbling and squealing. Taking her in my arms, I thanked God over and over for His goodness to me.

Saintman was still unsmiling. "I hope you've learned your lesson," he said sharply.

A familiar sickness gripped my stomach. The dancing in the night was no more. But GirlChild was in my arms, and God was in my heart. We headed for the car.

On the way back to the farm Saintman told me that he had meant for me to meet the wrong train. He had believers stake me out at the station to make sure that I had not called the police. If there had been any trouble, they were to signal him to keep hidden when he came on the next train.

And so we were reunited. Having no other alternative, we stayed in the area. Saintman found work with believers in a nearby city. In due time, I found myself pregnant again.

I remained obedient to Saintman, so he tolerated me fairly well. There was no love between us, but I didn't expect any. My mind was focused on GirlChild and learning all I could about God.

At the precise moment of the birth of our little son, Girl-Child ceased to be of any importance to Saintman. She did not take well to this and began behaving jealously, pinching the baby when he slept. Saintman disciplined her harshly, which only made her worse. I spent much of my time trying to ward off trouble between them.

Sometime the following year Saintman became enamored with pornographic literature. I found it hidden in a box of Christian pamphlets. Never having seen anything of this nature, I was horrified. I placed it in a neat pile on his desk with one of his three-by-five cards on top. On the card I wrote, "Whatsoever things are pure…"

He was furious when he found it and commanded me to leave his things alone. But it didn't end there. He sent away for some of the commodities offered in one of the magazines—things that he felt insured him greater satisfaction in our marital relationship.

There was only one problem. Me. Saintman's pursuit of sexual pleasure became my nightmare. Not only was I totally repelled by his manner and speech, what he attempted just plain hurt. When I pleaded with him to discontinue his new "techniques," as he called them, he became incensed, telling me that I was frigid. Whatever he called it, I simply could not comply with his demands. It wasn't long before he lost interest in me entirely. I was moved into the children's bedroom.

Any relief I experienced was short-lived. Saintman began tak-

ing BoySon into his bed at night. When I protested, he told
me that I was out of place. I didn't know what to do and wasn't
certain of the implications.

Saintman started staying out until early in the morning. He
said he was watching TV in a hospital in town. It seemed strange
to me that he would do this since he was so against television
and did not allow one in our home.

One night GirlChild became very ill. She had been feverish
for several days, but this was serious. I called the hospital and
asked that Saintman be paged, telling them that he was watching TV on one of the floor's waiting rooms. After a few minutes
I was informed that he was not there.

GirlChild grew worse. I finally summoned a neighbor to
drive me to the hospital where GirlChild received treatment in
an emergency room. When we returned home, Saintman was
there. He told me I must have just missed him.

Chapter Thirteen

"I Have Seen Thy Tears"

He was six-foot-four and when he talked to me he always sort of hunched over as if trying to come closer to my eye level. An unemployed welder and mechanic, he filled his front yard with several hollowed-out car bodies, their motors in various stages of repair. His lawn had long ago given up decorating the place. The front yard was a flattened mass of dirt and dry grass, stray pieces of metal, discarded engines, seals, and other unidentified car parts. He was Saintman's best friend— his crony, as Saintman called him.

Lean and undernourished, Crony was unschooled and naive, but genuine. About my age, he was unmarried and "looking." He became Saintman's friend while working on our "new" older car. Impressed by Saintman's feigned importance, Crony hung around the house a lot. He never noticed Saintman's ridicule of him and laughed good-naturedly at everything he said. Privately, Saintman referred to Crony as his "sidekick" because wherever Saintman went, Crony went too.

The doorbell rang one morning after Saintman left for work. Going to the front door, I was surprised to see Crony, who always came to the kitchen door. He just stood there for a moment, his frame slightly hunched over and looking like it had just been hung out to dry on his shoulders. Shuffling his feet, he raised one of his big hands in a semicircular motion and said, "Hi." He was smiling, but his face looked troubled.

"C'mon in, Crony," I said, wondering what this was all about. "Saintman's at work."

"I know." Crony's face began to redden, and he shoved what could fit of his hands into his pockets. "I just think you should know what's goin' on."

Crony didn't come in. He just stood there in the doorway and explained. He told me that Saintman had offered him a hundred dollars to get me to leave him. Saintman had a girl, somebody he'd met in a park somewhere. He wanted the three of them (Saintman, the girl, and Crony) to tour Europe "when this is all over."

When I asked Crony how Saintman expected him to get me to leave him, Crony got really mad and said something about Saintman's needing "Bible grounds." Then he got red all over again and said he just didn't do that kind of thing. Apologizing awkwardly, he started to walk away, saying he had to go. Then he stopped stone still and just looked at me.

"If you need any help," he said quietly, "you can count on me."

After he had gone, I sat down, stunned. How could anybody as religious as Saintman use such deceit and malice? He spent hours reading his Bible, and loved leading out in religious meetings.

As I sat there, I began thinking about Saintman's basic dishonesty. He stole things from the vacant house next door, saying, "They don't belong to anybody, anyway."

When he wasn't sick but wanted a day off from work without using up his vacation time, he made me call in sick for him so he wouldn't have to lie to his employers. He told me I wasn't really lying. I was just obeying him.

Once, when he attended a religious seminar that ran a couple of days into the following week, some older believers offered to make up his loss in pay for the workdays he'd missed. Saintman made the most of the opportunity, not by taking the money (he'd lost none) but by refusing the offer.

Tears just on the surface of his eyes, he drew himself up to his full height and said, "No, no. God will make it up to me. It was worth the sacrifice."

Of course he obtained some fame over the matter, and his story was repeated several times at meetings as an example of "dedication." Saintman instructed me to say nothing. God was getting the glory.

Ever since the night GirlChild ended up in the emergency room, I suspected Saintman was seeing other women. All doubt was erased from my mind when he continued to purchase prophylactics, which disappeared regularly from his sock drawer though we never slept together. That he felt a need to have "Bible grounds" to dump me was ludicrous. It was all a show so he could continue in good standing with other believers.

I knew I had grounds for divorce, but was reticent to take action. My children were both still babies and I had no education. I kept waiting for "God's will," but didn't know how to know what that was for sure. Crony's little speech only made me feel worse.

The next few months were terrible. Saintman became harsher than he'd ever been. I took to sleeping downstairs on the couch because I cried so much at night and I didn't want to frighten GirlChild.

Early one Sunday morning I awoke to the sound of the wind in the three giant cedars in front of our house. For some reason, Saintman was not home and the children were still asleep.

I always slept with my Bible, holding it close to my chest as if I could absorb God from it. Now I began paging through it, looking for something, *anything* that might give me comfort and guidance.

As I read here and there, I became more and more distraught. I didn't want to read stories about other people. I wanted God to speak to *me*! So I spoke to Him.

Oh Father! I just can't go on. I need to hear what you want to say to me. Do you talk to people today, the way you used to talk to them in Bible times? It seems to me that you'd want to, but I don't know how to hear you. I believe you speak to us through the stories in the

Bible, but is that all there is? I need you to talk to me. Somehow, talk to me!

The wind outside was noisy. I got up and went outside and looked up into the majestic branches of the cedars. They swayed and roared almost musically with the sound of the wind. The wind. It had always seemed to beckon me with secrets I could never quite understand.

With deep inner turmoil, I began to shout out loud to God.

I can only hear the wind! Oh God, I can only hear the wind!

Suddenly a thought came to me. In the Bible the Holy Spirit is likened to the wind.

I can "see" and hear wind, but don't know where it comes from or where it goes.

I shouted louder as gusts of wind threw my hair about my face.

Your Spirit touches me like the wind touches these trees! They feel the wind, and so do I. I hear it when it passes by. Let me hear you, through your Spirit. Oh Father, speak to me through your Spirit!

Running back into the house, I grabbed my Bible and held it against my chest.

This is your Word. Please speak to me through your Word, through your Spirit. Please!

Opening my Bible, I put my finger on a text and began to read.

"I have heard thy prayer, I have seen thy tears: behold, I will heal thee" (2 Kings 20:5).

I could not breathe. Reading the words over and over, I slowly sank to my knees. My words came slower, measured.

You are the living God. You are my Father. You have heard my prayer and seen my tears. You spoke to me! You said exactly what I needed to hear. But do you really mean that you will heal me? Does it mean what I want it so much to mean? How can I know—do I dare ask you after you have already spoken to me once?

I was breathing heavily, my hands gripping my Bible like a drowning man might grip an oar thrown in his direction. I closed the Bible carefully and continued praying.

Forgive me; I can't stop, now. I have to see if you are really speaking to me.

I opened my Bible again and read, "Within three years, as the years of an hireling" (Isaiah 16:14).

Disappointed and feeling totally foolish, I thought to myself, *I should have known better. God doesn't want us flipping through our Bibles like that.*

However, I had heard of God speaking to people in this manner on occasions of extreme need. I was in extreme need!

Turning back to 2 Kings I re-read the passage: "I have heard thy prayer, I have seen thy tears: behold, I will heal thee."

I knew that at the very least He had given me *this* text, but my eyes were drawn to the next sentence. "On the third day thou shalt go up into the house of the Lord."

What? On the third day? From my study of Bible prophecy I understood that a day could stand for a year. What had it said in Isaiah? "Three years, as the years of an hireling."

Was God giving me something to cling to, a kind of time span, so that I might survive the present, knowing that there was hope for the future? I had to make sure. I would rather know nothing than to have false hope. Once more I prayed.

Father, I will ask only this last time, like Abraham who dared to ask three times about his nephew Lot in Sodom. I am filled with awe to think that you, the great God of the universe, would converse with me. I must know. Are these words really for me? Are the three years for me? Oh Father, are you really telling me such things?

Opening my Bible, I read: "As thou hast believed, so be it done unto thee" (Matthew 8:13). I put my Bible down and began the day's chores. Nothing more needed to be said.

I was returning home late from a shopping trip a few days later when the bright headlights of a vehicle coming up behind me at a fast clip shone in my rear-view mirror. Since the road was narrow and winding, passing was not a safe option. I tried to speed up a little to accommodate the pursuing driver's obvious desire to hasten on to his destination. GirlChild and BoySon were asleep in the back seat.

The driver kept coming faster and faster until his lights looked like they were about to come through my back window. My heart was gripped with a strange fear. Something was wrong. It was almost as if he was trying to run me off the road entirely. With both hands on the wheel I negotiated the last few turns and signaled that I intended to turn left into our driveway. The lights pressed even closer.

Wrenching my car into the driveway, I was shaken to see the headlights still following me. My heart was beating so fast my throat ached. I heard Saintman's laughter. Turning, I saw him and Crony getting out of Saintman's pickup. Crony wasn't laughing.

Later, after I had put the children to bed, I asked Saintman why he had done it.

"Just wanted to test your reflexes," he answered nonchalantly.

The next day Crony called me while Saintman was at work. He apologized for being involved the night before. He'd pleaded with Saintman, saying that the children were in the car. He'd tried to get him to stop. He told me that he'd never seen a more diabolical expression on a man's face than when Saintman was bearing down on my car.

Crony didn't come around much after that. Saintman started making open accusations that Crony and I were "involved" with each other. He also insisted I was mentally ill and insinuated I probably needed hospitalization. Finally one night when he was railing at me, I had enough.

Standing up from the rather crouched position I was in with Saintman standing over me, I confronted him. I told him that his nights out were no mystery to me, that he was welcome to leave me at any time. I told him it was not healthy for BoySon to sleep with his father every night. It was not I who was an unfit mother; he was an unfit father. Period.

At first, Saintman was so taken by surprise that he just kind of slumped back on a staircase that led to where the children were playing. For the first time I saw fear in his face. It only lasted a few moments.

With great force, he got up and rushed at me, grabbing me. He began to threaten me and to shake me violently. Shoving me toward the front door, he opened it and threw me outside then slammed it shut and locked it. I heard GirlChild begin to cry.

It was cold outside and before long I was shaking from the inside. I was stricken with a sense of defeat and panic. Patterned responses clamored to be followed. Beg! Cry! Submit! I could hear the wind high above me in the cedars, reminding me of God's promise. I sat still and did not cry.

After a while Saintman opened the door and looked out. "Learned your lesson yet?" he snapped.

"Yes, I think I have," I answered.

I got up and walked past him into the house to where Girl-Child was standing. Saintman began talking about the possibility of our separation.

"If you leave," he said, "you can have GirlChild. I'll take Boy-Son."

GirlChild looked up quickly to me, to Saintman, then back down again, saying not a word.

"That's insane!" I answered angrily. "I could never choose between the children, and neither will you. They will not be divided."

"We'll see about that," Saintman sneered.

I picked GirlChild up and went upstairs to prepare the children for bed. She kept asking me if Saintman was going to take BoySon away.

I hushed her as best I could, but my own heart was raging.

Chapter Fourteen

The Year-long Prayer

In the end, it was concern for BoySon's well being that caused me to make my decision to leave Saintman. I suspected that Saintman was perverted. I simply could not subject BoySon to growing up in bed with his father. The possibility that Saintman might kidnap BoySon as he had GirlChild would have to be left in God's hands.

I retained a lawyer through the Legal Aid Society, and arrangements were made as to when and where I would flee. I knew that I dared not stay in our home because we were located out in the country fifteen miles in any direction to the nearest town.

One of the members of our church agreed to serve papers on Saintman. He was an older man with impeccable integrity. I was completely surprised by his response when I asked for his help.

"It'd be a pleasure!" he assured me. "The man's a scoundrel. You should have done this long ago!"

How had he known? I had said nothing.

And so I left Saintman and moved, temporarily, into a little "church house" located next door to a small chapel. Though I left behind almost everything I owned, for the first time in years I felt happy—even when a staunch believer called on me to tell me how I had sinned and turned my back on God when I left Saintman. She quoted Matthew 19:8: "Moses, because of the hardness of your hearts, suffered you to put away your [husband]."

I heard myself answer her: "Whose heart? What if it's *Saintman's* heart? What if it's because *he* will not allow God to change him?" She left clucking her tongue, telling me that I was misinterpreting the scriptures.

Though I sometimes felt very sinful indeed for leaving Saintman, I was convinced there was no other choice. I prayed about it a lot then went on struggling to make life happy for my children.

People seemed to fall over each other to help me. I was amazed to learn that most of the members of my church supported my decision.

Crony brought milk. Several times a week, he'd sneak a gallon of milk onto my porch before dawn. Though I never told him, my neighbors always saw him.

The day came when Saintman was given visitation privileges. No matter what I pleaded before the court, he was granted the right to see his children. I was sick with fear and begged God for protection.

Please, Father, do not let my children suffer. Anything else! Just keep my children safe.

For several weeks nothing happened. As planned, I moved out of the church house into a small, rat-infested place in town. I still remember standing in the kitchen at night holding an evaporated milk can over an opening in a wall, trying to bomb some of the larger rats. I never got any of them.

Persuaded by a dear older couple in the church, I finally obtained a washer and dryer that I had left with Saintman. He was furious, even though I explained that it was for the kids' sake, that it was easier for him to sit in a Laundromat than it was for two small children.

"You had no right!" he seethed, caring nothing for the children.

One night he showed up at my house with another of his

friends, a real "heavy." When I opened the door, he pushed past me into the house announcing, "We've come to get my washer and dryer!" Heavy followed him in, looking very sinister. Then a funny thing happened.

As soon as Heavy got into the front room, he noticed Older Couple. They were the ones who insisted I get the washer and dryer in the first place and had just brought me a kitchen table

"Mom! Dad! What are you doing here?" he asked incredulously.

"What are *you* doing here!" his mother retorted. "Son, we're ashamed to see you involved in this sort of thing!"

So intent was Saintman on his task that he was oblivious to all the subtleties happening around him. He didn't even see Crony, who had been enlisted by Older Couple to help carry the table in. Leaning up against a wall, Crony greeted Saintman.

"Hello, ol' buddy. Fancy meeting you here."

Crony, who was a big man, literally towered over Saintman, who was not very tall. Acknowledging Crony, Saintman headed for the laundry room. Crony simply moved sideways and blocked the doorway. At that point, Saintman, who looked like a street hoodlum, motioned for Heavy to join him.

"C'mon," he said meanly, "let's take him!"

Heavy, who had wilted considerably, looked miserable.

"Aw, let's go. Let's just go," he said.

"What's the matter, you scared?" Saintman retorted stupidly.

Heavy cast a doleful look at his mother, who glared back at him.

"Shame on you!" she said, shaking her head back and forth.

Heavy turned and walked out of the house leaving Saintman to face Crony all alone. Crony was leaning against the doorjamb, kind of lanky and loose, but ready. Saintman cleared his throat as if to say something, then apparently changed his mind. He turned and left. He never mentioned the washer and dryer to me again.

Before long it was Christmas time. I put up a little tree, but couldn't stand the thought, "not a creature was stirring, not even a…"

The children had a glorious time making cookies. BoySon, who was nearing his third birthday, looked much like a cookie himself he had so much colored sugar and flour in his hair and overalls! He sang a little song as he worked, looking up shyly from time to time.

"Oh, I am so happy, as happy as can be, for I have a mudder dear, that Jesus gave to me."

We sang Christmas songs and hugged and felt very whole. No matter how poor we were, we were together. Crony came Christmas Eve with a bag of toys. A stuffed teddy bear for BoySon that was exactly the same size as he was, and a pretty doll for GirlChild that said, "Mama." When I thanked Crony for his kindness he said it made Christmas for him too.

The divorce was to be final the third week in January. *It's almost over*, I thought to myself as I looked out at the freshly falling snow.

The kids were with Saintman that weekend. I wandered about the house feeling lonely and anxious. I always felt anxious when Saintman had the kids—always suffered when he brought them back later than usual. My church friends assured me that God would never allow Saintman to take the kids, reminding me that I must have faith.

Crony warned me, though, that he'd seen boxes stacked in Saintman's house. He'd gone to return something to Saintman, who slammed the door in Crony's face—but not before Crony had gotten a glimpse of the boxes.

What did it mean? And what could I do, anyway?

Looking at the snow, I prayed.

Oh Father, I'm so scared. I don't want anything to happen to the kids. Everyone tells me that you won't let anything happen, but I'm still frightened. Please don't let my lack of faith make any difference. I'm trying to believe. Please help me to believe. I'll do anything. Just don't let anything happen to my children.

It was getting dark. Saintman was almost an hour late. The snow was falling heavily now. That was it—the snow! He was late because of the snow! God wouldn't let anything happen. I had to have faith; everything depended on it!

Another half hour passed then the phone rang. Thinking it was Saintman, I was surprised to hear a woman's voice.

"Are you GirlChild's mother?"

"Yes," I answered, cold fear surging through my body.

"Your husband said you'd pick her up. He told me to call and remind you if you didn't show up."

"Do you have *both* my children?" I screamed into the phone.

"Both? Ma'am, your husband said that you'd pick up your little girl."

"Oh God!" I cried. "Please tell me, do you have my little boy too?"

After a pause, she answered how I feared she would.

"No, he left only your little girl. I didn't see a little boy."

It had happened—what everyone told me God would not let happen. I got directions to the woman's house and called the police. They told me to stay put, that they'd get GirlChild for me. They wanted to question the woman.

I waited alone in the silent house, hearing only the faint gnawing of a rat somewhere in the walls. Then I could stand it no longer. I ran out into the street. The snow was several inches deep and falling in a fairytale manner, softly, muffling the sound of a passing car. It could have been pretty. I yelled into the stillness, "Why?"

Why had God allowed this? What purpose was there in tearing us all apart? Saintman was not a good man. He was criminal, and somewhere in the darkness he was escaping with little Boy-Son. Oh BoySon! His birthday was less than a week away.

When the police brought GirlChild to me, she was unusually quiet. Only later did she cry, telling me that she had begged Saintman to take her with him. She couldn't understand why he took BoySon and not her. Not that she really wanted to be with

Saintman. She was wounded that she had been abandoned. And so, at the age of five and a half, she sustained a hurt that was a lifetime deep.

I knew that Saintman did not want to be married to me, so I had little hope that he would ever try for reconciliation. Never in my life did the world seem so large.

With GirlChild in my arms, I tried to steel myself against what I sensed was going to be a very long time. I knew that I would do everything possible to find BoySon, but I could not let GirlChild feel that I, too, would abandon her for him.

Forcing myself to focus on her, I told her how precious she was to me and that God must have known that I could never have stood it had she been taken too. She responded immediately and, in her own little way, tried to comfort me.

We went to stay at Older Couple's house for the next few days. Repeatedly excusing myself from their presence, I went to a back bedroom to cry, convulsed with grief. The police were of little help saying that they needed a lead before they could look for BoySon. Of course, there was no lead. My only hope was in God.

Oh God, I don't know where you are. I am so afraid that all this is happening because I made a mistake somehow, somewhere, but I don't know how or where. Too many people are telling me too many things, and I don't understand anything. But this I know: I said I'd never leave you again, and I won't. Please give me the strength to live. And please be with little BoySon! Don't let anything bad happen to him. If it is in your will, please bring him back to me. You are the only hope I have. I am clinging to you.

It was a good thing I had no idea how long I was going to have to cling. I heard nothing from Saintman for a year.

People who had been so sure that God would not allow Saintman to take the children had been equally sure that he would not be allowed to keep BoySon for long. After two months passed, however, they hardly knew what to say.

The police were almost indifferent. Although Saintman was formally charged with second-degree kidnapping, they openly admitted that they were not actively looking for him. It was up to me to find him. If I did, they would step in.

That did it. I became a tigress, fierce in the defense of her young, on the prowl for clues as to Saintman's whereabouts. I hired a private detective for a day using a full month's rent. He found nothing, but suggested that Saintman might be using an alias. Of course!

Saintman's birth certificate bore a different name than the name he assumed when his mother remarried. When I called his mother she told me the name, apologizing for the cruelty of her son.

Using every avenue I could think of, I learned that Saintman had obtained passports for both himself and BoySon, using his birth certificate name. Going to a U.S. Congressman's office, I obtained official help in blocking Saintman's passage out of the country. My next stop was a Senator's office. There my story was placed in a local newspaper with the hope that the Associated Press would pick it up. It was not.

I alerted income tax officials who agreed, unofficially, to co-operate if Saintman filed a return. A friend at the telephone company offered to unofficially give me copies of Saintman's past phone bills in hopes that any long distance calls he had made would give me a lead as to where he'd gone. I checked every number to no avail.

Some church members became suspicious that I was not everything they thought I was because of my continuing dilemma. My own thoughts churned, groping for some explanation. Night after night I was haunted with questions about myself and about God.

The months passed—four, five, then seven and eight. My nerves were shattered, my hopes shrunken into pygmy-like aberrations. Lying awake at night hugging BoySon's teddy, I listened. Sometimes I heard the drone of a distant plane, making my heart ache. Where was the plane going? Where was BoySon? My agony was parodied in the fading hum of the un-seen aircraft.

Ten months passed, then eleven. I cried until no more tears

came. It was like getting the dry heaves in my heart. I was being slowly driven down to the core of my existence—to where I would nakedly decide about God; where believing in Him offered no apparent reward.

It was primitive, almost sacred, for it was untouched by my emotions. My feelings would have demanded denial. Faith hadn't made the world work right. God hadn't done what He was "supposed" to do. But when I came to the core of my own heart I found that I still believed—in *God*, not in circumstances. He did not have to prove Himself to me by giving BoySon back to me. I simply trusted Him. It was settled.

GirlChild and I celebrated Christmas alone. On the eve of the anniversary of BoySon's kidnapping, I went out under the stars. It had been a very long year. I had never stopped praying for his return. "BoySon, I miss you!" I whispered.

Chapter Fifteen

Home at Last

GirlChild and I moved back to our home in the country. I called it Three Cedars because of the lofty trees in the front yard where God had promised me healing. Though my heart was in agony from the loss of BoySon, I tried to make life as normal and happy as possible for GirlChild.

One evening as I was preparing for bed I received an unexpected call from an acquaintance of several years back. He told me that he had to make something right. He told me that Saintman fled to his home when he first took BoySon a year ago. Saintman acted so strangely, however, that he and his wife became wary of him and insisted he leave. Ten months ago Saintman had headed south. My body tingled all over.

Ten months ago! I finally had a direction, though it did me little good now. A week later I received another unexpected call—from Saintman! He said he was tired of hiding and wanted me to drop the kidnapping charges so he could settle down and live a normal life with his son. My mind was reeling

"Please! Let me speak to BoySon!"

My throat was so tight I could hardly get the words out.

"No," Saintman replied in his deadly calm voice. "I have been teaching him to forget you. He doesn't talk about you anymore, and I don't want to get him upset."

BoySon doesn't talk about me anymore! I knew that I mustn't allow the full impact of these words to enter my heart, for they promised insanity. Instead, I begged Saintman to let little Boy-Son come to the phone. A new slyness came into Saintman's voice.

"If you drop the kidnapping charges, I'll let him talk to you."

I knew the game by now and told Saintman that I'd consider it. I was crying hard and pled with him to tell BoySon that I loved and missed him. He abruptly hung up.

For hours all I could think about were the years I had lived without assurance that my mother loved and missed me. I couldn't bear the thought that BoySon was experiencing the same hurt.

Then I had an idea. Quickly calling my next-door neighbor, whose unnamed friend at the phone company had helped me before, we worked out a plan to try to trace the next call from Saintman. There was only one catch. I had to let her know when Saintman called so she could alert Phone Company Friend.

There was also a logistical problem. Our houses were several hundred feet apart through a thicket of undergrowth. GirlChild was the only one who could make the journey. After careful consideration, we plotted the route she should take and enlisted her help.

Adventurous by nature, GirlChild took to the idea from the start. I think she was glad to be doing something to help bring BoySon home.

Then we waited, certain that Saintman would call again. Sure enough, he did. Though it was late at night, GirlChild awoke immediately when I touched her and went without murmur, flashlight in hand, to tell Neighbor.

Though I tried to keep Saintman on the line, he grew impatient with me and hung up before the call could be traced. However, we did discover through which large city his trunk line passed. Phone Company Friend told me I'd have to talk considerably longer if I hoped to pinpoint where he was.

Talk longer? Saintman and I had never talked very long. I asked God to help keep Saintman on the line the next time he called—if there was a next time.

About this time I learned that Heavy and his wife, who had always fawned over Saintman, were involved in Saintman's initial flight with BoySon. Not wanting to stir them up, I kept the information to myself.

Two weeks later, again late at night, Saintman called. I woke GirlChild as quietly as possible and dispatched her to Neighbor's.

Saintman seemed talkative, telling me about his girlfriend. She liked the beard he had grown. He asked about various believers, desiring "tidbits" as he called them, about their personal lives. I told him every thing I knew, and then got him talking about how clever he was to have avoided the police for so long. He loved thinking he was sly, and reminisced about his boyhood when he deliberately used to get the police to chase him. He could always lose them, and it gave him a thrill.

After a while he began badgering me to drop the kidnapping charges. I feigned weakness, asking him what assurance I had that he'd let me talk to BoySon if I complied with his wishes. At that point, he returned to his old pattern of dealing with me, growing increasingly impatient and abrasive.

I knew time was running out. Looking up, I saw Neighbor standing in my bedroom door, her large face ecstatic. "We've got him!" she mouthed.

Goose pimples shot up all over my body. I mustn't give anything away. I began pleading for Saintman to let me talk to Boy-Son. Angry now, he yelled at me that I'd never see my little boy again, and hung up.

Neighbor and I hugged each other and jumped up and down, crying and laughing as GirlChild stood by watching. I took her up in my arms and told her that she was a brave, wonderful little girl.

"Are we going to get BoySon back?" she asked breathlessly.

I could not answer her. The police had known about my "telephone connection" and told me that if I came up with anything to let them know, day or night. Neighbor already had taken care of this for me. Through her, I was told that all the machinery possible had been set in motion. They would probably have news for me in the morning.

I could not sleep that night. Frozen with anticipation, all I could do was pray, casting BoySon's name heavenward over and over and over. Each hour of the night passed like dehydrated glue being squeezed out of a plastic bottle.

Early the next morning the district attorney called to tell me that the police in the state where Saintman was located were closing in on him that very minute. When they had him for sure, I would be notified. I should be ready to leave immediately by plane to rendezvous with the authorities and pick up my son, thus avoiding the red tape of extradition.

Heavy's parents put up the money for tickets. I showered and dressed carefully, feeling like I was about to meet royalty. At ten o'clock that morning I got the call.

The district attorney was pleased to be able to tell me that they had apprehended Saintman without incident. BoySon was fine and in the process of being transported to the nearest metropolis where he would be taken to the airport to await my arrival.

I replaced the receiver and knelt by my bed to thank God for His goodness to me.

The ordeal was over. BoySon was coming home! Would he know me? Would he be afraid? It had been a year and twenty days since I'd last seen him. In that time he'd grown from a baby to a little boy.

My head was spinning as Heavy's parents drove me to the airport. The whole boarding process felt like a dream—floating down the ramp to the plane, taking my seat by the window, listening to the stewardess give instructions on what to do if our cabin's air pressure failed during our flight.

I was sure that, should the plane go down, my heart would keep me flying all the way to BoySon!

The sky was overcast and gray, and little droplets of water

trekked slowly sideways across my window. Abruptly the plane burst through into the sunshine. It startled me. I had never thought about there being sunshine above the clouds. Instantly, the significance hit me, and I started to laugh. Turning to my seatmate, a rather dour businessman type, I giggled almost uncontrollably. "The sun's shining!" I said.

Obviously used to flying, he looked at me condescendingly. Returning to his newspaper he muttered, "Of course. It's been that way ever since creation."

"Before creation!" I said, knowing that it didn't make a bit of sense to him, and knowing that I wasn't talking about the hot star that warmed our planet.

God's Son has been shining above our darkened world since forever. My occasional feeling that He was not there did not change the reality of His presence. By faith I could break through clouds of ignorance, grief, and sin to bask in the warmth of knowing Him.

My eyes were as full of sky as my mind was of God. How many times I had suffered in the night when I heard a plane I could not see traveling to where I did not know! Now somebody else far below heard the drone of *my* plane—a plane that was carrying me to my little boy!

The stewardess came to hand out snacks. I hadn't eaten since the day before. As I tore my package open I was shaking so hard that I spilled them all over my dour seatmate.

"Excuse me!" I said, obviously still full of laughter.

He picked the oily goobers off his clothing and moved as far away from me as possible. I was too happy to be properly contrite and took to my window once again.

Soon the captain announced our impending arrival. My stomach lurched. I had purchased a little metal replica of an airliner for BoySon and pulled it out of my purse as the plane's wheels hit the runway.

There was nobody at the gate that I recognized when I got off the plane, so I followed the crowd down a long corridor to some escalators. Lightheaded, I stepped on and began my descent to the main area of the terminal. Halfway down I saw him. His hair was long, like a girl's, but his face was BoySon's! He was sitting on a bench between a man and a woman.

Our eyes met and locked. One chubby little finger extended from somewhere under his jacket as he pointed me out to his escorts.

The man and woman looked up at me, but my eyes were on BoySon. Reaching the main floor, I held out the little metal plane as I approached him. Kneeling beside his bench, I fought back the tears. I must not frighten him. He took the plane and smiled.

"Are you...?" the woman began.

"BoySon," I said softly, "I've come to take you home."

BoySon stood up, wrapped both his arms around my neck, and whispered the most precious word I had ever heard.

"Mudder!"

He knew me! No matter what Saintman tried to do he could not erase from this little boy's heart the knowledge of his mother! And such a little gentleman he was! Though dressed in his sister's old flowered jacket and pair of boots, he had about him a dignity that went straight to my heart.

We had several hours of waiting before our plane was to take us home. We walked around and got something to eat. I could not take my eyes off my son. He talked a blue streak, noticing everything. The sound of his voice was balm to my heart.

Finally it came time to board our plane. I picked BoySon up and started down the ramp. He hid his face in my neck, pulled my long hair over his head, and murmured something.

"What?" I asked.

"Don't ever leave me again," he said.

Chapter Sixteen

Square One All Over Again

My mother was among those who met us at the airport when BoySon and I arrived home. A friend of mine fetched her, knowing how much it would mean to me to have family there. She looked tired and anxious and a little self-conscious around my extended family of believers. I think it was then I began to realize that her relationship to me was ruined more by her own insecurities than by some defect in myself.

It was a strange, fleeting moment. I wanted to reach across the gulf between us and pull her close to me, but people were pushing in around us. GirlChild, eyes wide with curiosity, needed to be drawn in quickly and securely.

"Mommy! He's so big!" she said as BoySon peeked out at her from behind my veil of hair that he continued to make his refuge. He giggled, she giggled, and life began again.

At last we arrived home. GirlChild took BoySon on a tour, reintroducing him to once familiar objects and to toys that had been purchased for him "just in case" he had come home by Christmas. She explained how I had marked his presents with red dots so she could tell they were his, knowing that they were hers in his absence. At that, a little skirmish ensued as to ownership now that he *was* home. Somehow, it felt good to hear their little tempers clash. Everything was going to be just fine!

Spring arrived with a flourish of green. The children loved making mud pies in the garden to the side of the house, or building elaborate road systems in the dirt on which their little wooden people traveled.

We adopted two gray-striped kittens, Nip and Tuck, who tumbled and tussled in the grass. Little did I dream that Saint-man had gone before a judge, convincing him to free him "on his honor" until time for his extradition and trial.

Though I always was watchful when the children were outside, I didn't want them to live in a prison of fear as I had. My intention was to put all our troubles behind us, to live a normal life. Surely we had experienced the worst that could happen. Lightning never strikes twice.

I had just checked on the children when the phone rang. It was my neighbor. We had chatted only briefly when the front door flew open and GirlChild burst inside.

"He's got him! He's got him!" she screamed.

Instantly I was on my feet and out the door. Saintman was just leaping the ditch at the side of the road, BoySon clutched in his arms. I kicked off my shoes and raced across the grass.

"Mommy! Mommy!" BoySon cried over Saintman's shoulder.

Saintman snatched away a wig he was wearing and yelled to BoySon, "It's me, Daddy!"

Later BoySon told me, "I *knew* who it was!" But for now all he could do was cry out, "Mommy! Come get me!"

I fell and cut my knee on the rough edge of the blacktop as I cleared the ditch. By the time I got on my feet again the gap between us had widened considerably. BoySon's arms were outstretched over Saintman's back; his voice was more frantic than ever.

"Mommy!"

Feeling a sudden surge of strength, I ran faster than I could ever have imagined possible. The gap lessened.

"Stop!" I screamed. "Stop! I'll do anything!"

None of us really knows what we'll do in a crisis. I found myself yelling at the top of my voice simultaneously to Saintman and to God

"Stop!"

"God! Stop him!"

"Saintman, I'll marry you!"

"Help! God!"

I almost could feel my cries rupture heaven.

As we passed my neighbor's driveway I only had time to scream, "Help!"

She never saw me. She was still clutching her telephone receiver, yelling, "What's the matter? Are you all right?"

Terrified, GirlChild slammed and locked the front door, fleeing to an upstairs window to see what was happening. Later, only after much consoling, could the police get her to unlock the door. Then, seated on the leg of one of the three huge helicopters that were sent to begin searching for us, she answered questions as television cameras rolled.

"He tried to get me too," she said, though that was more her fear than it was Saintman's intention.

As I ran to catch Saintman, he reached a gravel road that wound behind some neighboring houses. I caught up to him a few feet onto the road and grabbed, first for Saintman's arm, then for BoySon. In a second I had my arms around BoySon's body. Saintman would have to kill me before I'd let go!

Cursing, he demanded I release the child.

"Mommy!" BoySon cried, and I hung on.

Soon we were out of sight of the main road. Saintman swung around knocking me to the ground with BoySon. Grinding my arms and shoulders into the gravel with his boot, he swore at me, but BoySon and I held on to each other.

Perhaps because he was reluctant to take further action in front of BoySon, Saintman stopped trying to pull BoySon from me and jerked me to my feet.

"All right, then, you'll have to go with us," he hissed.

Like a wounded little bear, BoySon pulled my hair over his head and wrapped his arms and legs around my body.

Saintman locked his fingers around my arm like a vise grip as he led us to his car a little distance ahead. My feet made scraping sounds as they dragged on the gravel. The forest, uncommitted, seemed to watch as we passed, walling us in to tragedy. In my heart I continued crying out to God.

I don't understand. Where are you? Where are you?

Opening the car door, Saintman shoved us inside, then went around to the other side and got in. Only when he started the motor did I fully realize that nobody was going to stop him. My heart froze.

Why? was all I could pray.

Back on the main road we traveled for maybe an hour. Saintman pulled onto an old logging road. Back, back into the darkening woods we drove until the road thinned out to nothing. Stopping the car, Saintman commanded me to get out. BoySon was hysterical.

"No, Mommy, no!" he screamed.

Reaching for a rope in the back seat, Saintman once again ordered me out of the car.

"You'll have to kill me," I said. "Kill me right in front of Boy-Son!"

Saintman endeavored to comfort BoySon, explaining that I'd be all right. He was going to tie me to a tree, just to keep me from following them. Men would come soon and set me free.

"The tree and God and me in one final, fatal embrace," I thought to myself.

"The bears will get her!" BoySon cried, clinging to me desperately.

Saintman threw the rope into the back seat and got out. Going to the rear of the car, he changed the license plates, bragging that he'd lifted them off a car parked along a street somewhere.

As he worked, I talked softly to BoySon, telling him that God knew where we were. He begged me not to leave him. Saintman appeared in the door.

"Get out, both of you. We're going to have prayer."

I stared at Saintman in disbelief.

"We're going to ask God to be with us, to reunite our family. You are going to promise Him that you will keep your promise to marry me and that you will not try to get anyone to interfere."

The whole idea was utterly ludicrous, but Saintman was dead serious. I had screamed that I'd marry him again, and he was taking me up on my offer!

Why, oh why, in my desperation, had I cried out such a foolish thing? Confusion flooded my mind. Saintman knew that I never lied, and he was counting on that now. He was also counting on my devotion to God. He would make me repeat my promise to God as a surety that I would go through with it. He understood my simpleness, my naiveté. And I misunderstood divine perspective. How God must have wept for me that day!

Getting out, we knelt in the shadows of the forest around us—shadows so dense that light from the dome in the car formed a halo on the ground where we knelt. The ground was soft with an undisturbed accumulation of pine needles. Their fragrance rose up to me, as if to anoint my heart in an hour of sorrow.

Saintman told me what to say: "I will never leave you again. I promise to keep this pledge. I will not try to get help."

I wept as I spoke the words, and added, "Father, I've never lied to you. Please help me to keep this pledge!"

In my mind, though, I qualified my words.

I said I'd never leave YOU, again. Help me to never lose faith in you, no matter what happens!

Satisfied, Saintman prayed, "Witness these things, oh God!" and then uttered a loud "Amen."

We got back into the car, turned it around and took up our journey. BoySon, exhausted, fell asleep in my arms almost immediately. We emerged from the woods onto the main road and eventually came to a familiar town bright with fast-food restaurants. At a stop sign I saw a large, lanky man in a phone booth.

Crony! Or was it? It didn't matter. He never saw our car.

I repeated Saintman's words as a prayer in my mind.

Witness these things, oh God. But why are you letting these things happen? I'm sorry that I yelled that I'd marry Saintman. Will you hold me to this? God, please don't hold me to it! Please, please don't let Saintman get away with this!

My mind turned to GirlChild. How frightened she must be! *Please be with little GirlChild. Comfort her and keep her safe. Will I ever see her again? Oh God, I'm so tired. Where are you? How can you let this happen?*

Night had fallen when, some hours later, Saintman again pulled off the highway and up a gravel road into the mountains. The road ended in a clearing adjacent to a railroad track. The rails gleamed in the moonlight.

"We'll sleep here," he announced.

Revulsion hit me as he lowered the back seat to make a bed. Crawling into the space, I laid our sleeping son between us.

"Don't try anything," Saintman warned, "or you'll never see your son again! Besides, you promised God, remember?"

A little while later I told Saintman that I needed to make a trip outside. He grunted as I slipped out the door and into the cold night air. Knowing he would expect it, I crouched down, but instead of staying in one spot I crawled to the back of the car and read the license plate. I tried to memorize it, but my mind was like a sieve.

Please, help me!

A little jingle formed in my mind, the first letter of each word matching the letters on the plate. I've long since forgotten the rhyme, but it was about GirlChild being left behind. Crawling back to the car door, I got in and repeated the rhyme again and again, singsong, until dawn.

Morning came, parting the trees with shimmering light. I sat up, beholding the day. How long is eternity? How can I possibly be in this car with little BoySon huddled up against me as if trying not to touch Saintman? Saintman was just waking up. The sight of him made me sick. BoySon awoke. For an instant he looked terribly startled, but he never said a word.

"Want some granola?" his father offered.

BoySon looked up at me questioningly. I nodded to him. He would need nourishment for the day ahead.

"We'll have worship before we eat," Saintman declared.

I felt like throwing up as he opened his Bible and began reading aloud.

"Please don't read aloud." My voice was almost a whisper.

With a look of pious disgust, he just nodded. "That should tell you something about yourself."

I lowered my head.

I'm sorry. I just can't. Not now. Not here, and not from him.

"I gotta go potty!" BoySon interrupted.

"Sure, Daddy will take you, just like old times!" Saintman said with a grin.

Scooping up BoySon, he headed for the bushes, taking the car keys with him. On the seat beside me was a wig he had used the day before to kidnap BoySon. It was an ugly, repulsive thing, like an animal! On an impulse I grabbed it, leaned out the open door, and threw the hairy mass under the car. Leaning back against the seat I started to laugh, wondering what the person who found it (if anybody did) would think.

My eyes came to rest on Saintman's open Bible. A pencil rested in its binding—he always marked texts as he read. Did I dare? My hand slowly went for the pencil. Having no pockets, I slipped the pencil inside my pants.

From your Word this morning, Father. Now I need some paper.

My eyes were drawn to the floor in front of me. I leaned over and felt under the seat. My fingers touched a scrap of paper. I drew it out: a discarded grocery slip. Down it went inside my pants.

Thank You, Father. Tell me when.

Picking up Saintman's Bible, I held it briefly to my breast, then, hearing him return, I lowered it.

"Hope it does you some good," Saintman said sarcastically.

"I do too." I replied.

Chapter Seventeen

In God's Name

Try as I might to stifle the feeling, from deep inside of me there came a moaning that I could not stop. Up, up, and out it came from the pit of my misery, across my wounded heart, and through my aching throat like a primeval cry. I pressed my mouth against my arm to muffle the sound, while rivers of tears ran down my face, soaking my sleeve.

My crying irritated Saintman.

"Shut up!" he commanded. "It won't do you any good to cry those crocodile tears!"

Several times he pulled to the side of the road and threatened to push me out. Each time BoySon threw his little arms around my neck from behind and pleaded that I be allowed to stay. Relenting, Saintman's angry eyes would cut at me like switch-blades.

Our journey took us across many miles of barren terrain—no trees, no houses, scarcely a sign of human life. Our car passing by barely broke its bleak monotony. Even the sky seemed bored with clouds forming aimless patterns on its deep blue background.

My moaning finally ceased in a final spasm. BoySon was asleep, one arm thrown protectively up against my left shoulder. My mind felt limp as I groped for God.

I know the universe is a big place. Maybe you are busy somewhere else. I feel abandoned, not because you don't love me, but

because there must be more important things you need to tend to.
Please, though, I hope you can find time to help me. I need you so
desperately.

Even though such a thought wounded me to the core of my
soul, it did not seem unfair to me that God might be too busy to
deal with my situation. People who are born into material poverty rarely break through their learned lifestyle patterns. Generation after generation of ghetto families rise no higher than did
their parents. I had been born into emotional poverty, as had my
mother and her mother before her. Unintentionally, I brought
this mentality with me into my spiritual life: I expected not to
count for much.

God had promised to heal me. Instead, it seemed that I had
been delivered directly into the hands of the very one who meant
to utterly destroy me. It confused and distressed me beyond my
ability to reason. Like a slum child, I hated my life but ended up
picking through "rubbish" for sustenance because I didn't know
what else to do—and expected nothing better.

I wanted to be physically free from Saintman. God wanted
to free me from emotional poverty. I barely hoped for immediate deliverance. God knew I needed a far deeper and more permanent deliverance. He was not "somewhere else," too busy to
notice my plight. By taking a little longer, He would give me my
first sure step out of my spiritual ghetto. Meanwhile, He would
have to leave me to pick through my inadequate understanding
of Him.

Up ahead a rest stop came into view. We pulled off the road
and stopped in the middle of a deserted parking area.

"Don't you dare try anything," Saintman snarled as I got out
and headed for a rest room. I entered the building and noted
that it was as bleak inside as it was outside. Cement block walls,
concrete floor, a bare sink, and two doorless stalls.

I reached into my pants and retrieved the pencil and grocery
slip. Kneeling on the floor, I scribbled these words: "Help! This
is not a joke. My little boy and I have been kidnapped. Please
contact the sherriff."

Not realizing it at the time, I misspelled "sheriff." I finished the note: "Blue station wagon, license plate number..." I paused. Oh, what was it? Singsong, singsong—oh, what was that rhyme? GiriChild's face came to my mind, and I filled in the letters, signed my name, and looked for a good place to hide the note.

"Barren, sterile place, have you no womb?" I spoke urgently, scanning the room.

My eyes came to rest on a towel machine. A continuous loop of linen hung limply from its container. I wet my hands at the lavatory and dried them on the towel so that it looked wet, then folded my message and slipped it up just inside the machine's lip. The next user would receive toweling and my note!

Sticking the pencil back inside my pants I returned to the car. Saintman immediately entered the restroom to see if I had tried to leave some kind of message. He came out and told BoySon and me to get back into the car. I wondered, as we pulled away, how long it would be before another woman would stop there.

As we neared a large city, Saintman switched on the car radio. I was amazed to hear my name and BoySon's in connection with a three-state search by the police.

Saintman smiled and flexed his driving arm rhythmically back and forth as he listened. I turned my face to the window. Cars sped past us. I called to the drivers with my eyes, but they could not know.

Later that afternoon, Saintman switched the radio off as we pulled into a gas station. When I told him that I needed to use the restroom he nodded, warning me that if I tried anything I would never see BoySon again.

As I started for the building the pencil began sliding down my pant leg. I pressed my knees together to stop its progress, groaned and put my hand over my stomach. Perhaps it would fool him into thinking my strange walk was appropriate.

"For crying out loud, hurry up!" he jeered.

My ruse had worked!

I barely made it inside before the pencil hit the floor. It would have been a comedy if it weren't so serious. Looking quickly about, I spotted a piece of paper in an overflowing trashcan. I wrote a second note, again misspelling "sherriff." Time was running out and this time there was no towel machine. At terrible risk, I decided to leave the note in plain sight. Placing it carefully on the trash can lid, I went out, letting the door slam and lock behind me.

"Hey!" Saintman shouted.

I feigned meekness. "Oh, I'm sorry. I'll go get the key."

Hesitating a moment, he waved me back to the car. "Forget it. We need to get going."

We drove into a large city. Saintman told me there were wedding chapels where people could get married the same day they got a license. We'd have to find a courthouse and get a marriage license.

Looking at my bare feet, I wondered what people would think when we applied for a marriage license. As it turned out, nobody even noticed!

First came blood tests. My blood cried out, but no one heard.

At the courthouse we left BoySon alone in the car. Saintman warned me that if I tried to alert anyone, he'd escape in the confusion and I'd never see the child again. It was enough to keep me in line. I wasn't sure how people would react, and I knew that if I blew it, I might not have another chance. Still, I pleaded for help with my eyes.

People must have thought I was on drugs.

At last we approached a small wedding chapel. A sign hung over its doorway—Marriages. It could have said anything—hardware, furniture, slaughterhouse. A woman sitting in the window watched us as we walked toward the building. I mouthed, "Help!" as I followed Saintman inside. Apparently my face had melted away. The lady smiled.

"We want to get married," Saintman stated coldly.

The woman smiled again. Lipstick showed on her front teeth. Soon we were joined by another woman who led us into the chapel portion of the little house. I mouthed, "Help!" to her, too, but she never batted an eye.

Oh God! Am I invisible? Can't they see that something is terribly wrong? Am I going insane? Have I no eyes, no face, no soul?

A moment later the ceremony began. All those familiar words.

"Dearly beloved, we are gathered here..."

God, where ARE you? Am I invisible to you, too? How can this be happening? Please don't let it happen!

I began to cry freely. It didn't matter anymore. I didn't care what Saintman thought. I didn't care what the woman performing this obscene ceremony thought. I felt deserted by God though for what reason I could not fathom. All I knew was that, with each word uttered in this room, I was being sealed into a tomb as black and deep as hell itself—all in the name of God!

The woman's voice rose dramatically. It must have been her thing, her way to achievement, to be able to stand in the position of a minister of God marrying people. How could she miss my agony? Oblivious to my grief, she was obviously enjoying herself immensely.

I felt hot shame for her, for myself, and for the whole ludicrous affair. And somewhere in all this was God. How could He look upon such a scene? I felt that any knowledge I might have had of Him was gone—gone in this open rape of my conscious being.

"Do you take this woman...?"

I heard Saintman say, "Yes."

"And, do you take this man...?"

Anger welled up in me like a terrible dragon. Was I supposed to submit to this disregard of human dignity? Was my mouth to confirm what every cell in my body abhorred? Saintman's fingernails dug cruelly into my hand, and I wanted to scream, "No!"

BoySon's face flashed into my mind. Fear ripped through my heart. I quickly cried, "Yes!"

It was done.

"You may kiss the bride," the woman said, sounding rather

pleased with her progress. Involuntarily, I turned my face away from Saintman.

"We'll take care of that later," he said flatly.

As she pronounced us man and wife, I collapsed.

"No, no, no, no, no..." my voice trailed off to a whisper.

It was done. I had been recaptured, shot through the heart with a poison dart. There was no strength left in me.

Someone helped me to the next room and onto a couch. I wept softly, with no hope. There was no one who could help me now.

"Poor little bride," intoned the lady with lipstick on her teeth as she stroked my forehead. "Poor little bride."

Handing Saintman a certificate, the lady minister assured him that I'd be okay. He grunted, then pulled me to my feet, saying we'd better get back to the car. I stumbled after him, only wanting to get back to BoySon.

"I must live for him," I thought, "and for GirlChild."

Back at the car, BoySon's tear-streaked face was pressed against the window

"Mommy, Mommy!" he cried over and over as we got back into the car.

"I'll never leave you again," I soothed him as we drove out of town.

"Not quite true," Saintman said coolly.

Naming a metropolis a few hours away, he informed me that when we arrived, he would put me on a bus for home. I was to go to the police and make sure that all charges against him were dropped. He'd contact me later time to make sure that everything was in order. Then we could be reunited.

So. I'd paid the price and lost anyway. I knew Saintman had no intention of reuniting with me. I had just completed a ceremony that insured noninvolvement by any law enforcement agency. Married to Saintman, I had given him legal custody of BoySon. The despised marriage certificate lying on the dashboard was his ticket to freedom.

"You've won," I said. "Do this one thing for me. Take me

back to the town we just came from so I can get home to Girl-Child sooner. She must be sick with worry, and I am so tired. You've won. Just let me go."

Evidently feeling that I spoke quite accurately, Saintman agreed. There was no doubt he wanted to be rid of me. As he turned the car around, I reached for the certificate and unrolled it. Besides our names written at the top, it was blank. No one had signed it—neither Saintman nor I, or the lady minister! The spark of hope was tiny but powerful, hitting my heart like an electric shock. Throwing the certificate into the back of the car so Saintman would not look at it, I reached for BoySon and took him into my arms.

Saintman drove me directly to a bus station. Though BoySon was crying hard, I allowed Saintman to pull him from me as I got out of the car.

"Don't cry, BoySon. I will be with you soon!" I promised, not daring to question my own heart as to the verity of this.

Turning quickly, I walked straight toward the bus station without looking back. Stumbling through the door I fell across the counter.

"Call the police!" I said. "And please hurry; my little boy and I were kidnapped. It's been on the radio."

Chapter Eighteen

Rescue!

The ticket man whirled around.

"Call the police!" he yelled to a man nearby.

He rushed to pull me into a back room in case Saintman should return. I heard some of the waiting passengers offering descriptions of Saintman's car.

Sitting alone in a coatroom waiting for the police to arrive I sat unmoving on a straight-backed chair and prayed fervently.

Dear God, I beg of you, have pity on us! I'll do anything you want. Just bring BoySon back to me! I'll go to the farthest corner of the world and sit there quietly for the rest of my life. I'll never bother you again.

As if that's what God wanted—a slave's bargain! As though BoySon's well-being were not as much His concern as it was mine! Nonetheless, I felt beggarly and unworthy, and was willing to accept even spoiled crumbs from the Master's table.

Soon the police arrived. Kind officers probed me with questions. I was so tense that I felt as though all my veins were being shortened, constricting the free movement of my body parts. They told me someone found my note in the gas station restroom. Even before the bus station notified them, the police decided my note was genuine because I misspelled the word sheriff.

I was informed that every highway patrol unit within 200

miles was alerted. They were all converging on the area. A huge net was being dropped.

"We'll get him!" I was as assured. "It's only a matter of time."

A half hour passed. People moved about and talked of this and that. My brain felt stuffed with cotton, making me dreamlike and far-removed from the ordinary room in which I sat. I caught myself wringing a tissue someone had given me, and stopped immediately. It seemed like such an artificial thing to do—something heroines did in the movies.

I felt stupid, like I was pretending or something. A familiar, disgusted voice sounded in my mind. "Hypocrite! You're being melodramatic! You're mentally sick!"

My face turned crimson.

"But this is *real!*" I said out loud, my own voice an argument.

Oh God, what does one act like in situations like this?

As soon as I made it a three-way conversation—the mental voice, my own audible voice, and my prayer to God—the accusations stopped. My body relaxed and I threw the tissue into a garbage can under the desk. The room came into focus.

Suddenly everyone seemed to jump up and rush about. "They've got him! Just across the state line!" Everyone cheered.

I was given a phone and directed to talk to the district attorney back where I lived.

"Take it easy, Sweetheart," he said. "We'll take care of everything from here on out. And don't worry about your bogus marriage. It won't stop due process. Your little son should be back to you in a few minutes. We've been worried about you, you know. Never stopped looking for you for a moment. Things are going to be okay now."

Sure enough, a few minutes later BoySon arrived at the station. Rushing forward to greet me, he raised my hand to his lips like a miniature prince.

"My precious little Mommy!" he said.

I could not dismantle his dignity and so accepted his formal greeting. I wanted to grab him and cover him with kisses. But this time *he* was in control. I was so proud of him!

One of the officers told me what happened. Evidently Saintman stopped the car to change his license plates after dropping me off at the bus station. However, as he began to drive, the description given the police by those waiting at the bus station enabled a patrolman to spot his car. Saintman was pulled over, but produced a false I.D.

It almost worked except that BoySon, who had been told to hide under a pile of blankets on the floor of the front seat, could not resist the urge to see "a real policeman." He popped up, wide-eyed, just as the officer turned to go.

"Why, hello, young man!" the policeman greeted him. "And what is your name?"

Saintman had taught BoySon a false name for more than a year, but now he spoke distinctly, and with obvious pride, the name I'd told him was his own.

"Want to ride in my patrol car?" the officer asked.

"Yeah!" BoySon replied eagerly.

"I'll take you to see your Mommy!" the officer continued.

Looking at Saintman, he said, "And you, Sir, are under arrest."

Saintman offered no resistance.

BoySon and I were taken to a hotel near the police station for the night. Guards were posted downstairs just in case Saintman had accomplices. As I lay in the dark listening to BoySon's breathing, I was filled with a desire to keep him from further harm. GirlChild, too.

The awareness that, as yet, I had been unable to keep them from harm stung me bitterly. I called on God to protect us, but it seemed to make little difference. Or did it? BoySon was sleeping safely beside me. Why hadn't God prevented our abduction?

Was it in some way my fault? Had I misunderstood the teachings of the Bible? What did God expect from believers, anyway? How would I ever know? My feelings were uncertain, like I had secured the favor of a huge, celestial Lion—but was He always friendly? Was He always tame?

Whatever the case, I knew the only hope I had in life was in Him. I determined to try my best to obey Him so that He would find no displeasure in me that could possibly put my children in jeopardy. The scary part was that I was not exactly sure what brought on God's displeasure. Sin, for sure. But the concepts of sin and righteousness often got thrown around in religious discussions with such impunity that it left me wary of God. Was it not my task to untangle correctly this mish-mash of religious thought and come up with correct answers and actions that sufficed the inspection of Heaven?

I lay my head on the pillow next to BoySon.

Thank You, Father, for bringing BoySon back to me. I do not know what lies ahead, but I know that somehow you are in it all. As I search my heart, I cannot find that I am holding anything back from you.

Rolling onto my back, I made the motions of opening my garments before the Lord.

Look inside me, Father. See all that I cannot see. I give all the permission I know how to give for you to search me through and through. Let the darkest places in me and in my mind be filled with your light. Sometimes I am afraid of you, but you are all I have. I would rather take my chances with you than with the kindest man on the face of the earth.

Memories of God's love flooded my soul. The beauty of the natural world seemed to press in upon me even in the dark, dingy hotel room. A poignant desire for life and the Giver of life swelled in me until my heart strained for release from all the sorrows that tethered it. And clearly, so clearly— though without the benefit of satisfied reason— I knew that God accepted me; that whatever wrong thinking was left in me was under the full blaze of His presence, and that everything was all right.

The rest of my prayer was as much without words as was God's response. It went far deeper than words could go. It was *being.*

The next few weeks blur in my memory into a mass of court proceedings, endless advice from well-meaning friends, and a frustrating sense of futility. Saintman had warned me during our long drive over the barren countryside that if he was caught it would only be a matter of time before he returned to "finish the job."

I shuddered, thinking of his words: "They can bury me in the darkest hole in earth, but sooner or later I'll come back. And next time I won't fool around."

His words were like a death sentence. I knew he meant it. He was a real-life nightmare, like the "thing" in your dreams that defies killing and repeatedly comes after you.

One day the district attorney called me. Saintman was scheming for release into the custody of Heavy and his wife! I told the district attorney all that I knew concerning this couple of dubious charity. Together we laid a plan to thwart Saintman's endeavor.

The day of the hearing, I was quietly brought into the rear of the courtroom. Unaware of my presence, Saintman made quite a show before the judge. He assumed a stance of wounded nobility, his face the picture of abused innocence—a regular, clean-cut young man whose only crime was his passionate fatherhood. Clemency seemed the order of the day.

Saintman's voice quivered as he explained to the judge that he meant no harm by his actions. Dropping his head, he sobbed ever so lightly, letting his tears fall unchecked to the floor. His attorney took up his plea, stating that prison was totally alien to such a decent young man, that he should be released into the custody of good church folk who were friends of the family.

The district attorney, who was sitting nearby, approached the bench. "Your Honor," he began, "I have some additional information that should be taken under consideration before you grant the request at hand."

Saintman stiffened.

"Saintman's wife is present for questioning," the district attourney said. "She is opposed to Saintman's release to this particular family."

Saintman turned and looked at me. His hands clenched into fists, and a look of pure hatred hardened his face. He looked like a criminal who could easily commit a violent crime. The judge, who was watching Saintman, saw it all. The district attorney went on to give the details, which I had supplied.

"Are all these facts true?" The judge's tone had changed.

When Saintman refused to answer, the judge was abrupt.

"It is no small thing to try to pull the wool over the court's eyes. Request denied!"

Just the same, a few weeks later Saintman was released. He received what is termed a "sundown sentence." Having plea-bargained, his offenses was so reduced that he was left with only a minor charge of taking BoySon out-of-state overnight.

He was told he had twenty-four hours in which to leave the state where the children and I resided. He could choose his destination. A parole officer would be appointed at that locality to monitor his activities over the next five years. During this time he was not to contact us in any way, not by letter, not by phone, and certainly not in person.

He chose to return to the state in which he had been living with his girlfriend. It was her car that he was driving when he kidnapped BoySon and me!

I was stunned. Since when had Saintman ever kept his word? Did they actually believe he would obey parole? But since all the facts that could have been used to prove his lawlessness were non-admissible by reason of plea-bargaining, the court's decision was made accordingly.

It was I, for all practical purposes, who received a sentence for the next five years— a sentence of unrelenting fear. It was almost more than I could handle.

Every tree became his ambushment, every stranger a potential menace. The children did not want to play outside, and I wouldn't have let them had they wanted to. I could not sleep at night. Prayer did not help. I had no assurance that God would prevent Saintman's return; He hadn't prevented him the first time.

One night I heard sounds like someone walking on the lower roof of our tri-level home. I held my breath. There it was again! What could I do?

I slipped out of bed and down the stairs to the dining room. Peeking out a window, I saw nothing. If it was Saintman, I was sure he would not come alone. He was too much of a coward.

Suddenly I saw a flash of light. A flashlight! What shall I do?

I heard a rumbling sound overhead. Another flash of light followed, and more rumbling sounds. I reached for the phone. Then it came to me—thunder and lightning!

My knees buckled and for a moment I sat on the floor laughing helplessly with relief. Then I stopped. This wasn't funny. Saintman knew exactly where we were. We had to get out of this house. We were sitting ducks!

Chapter Nineteen

Wonderful Husband

I was running scared, desperately trying to hold onto hope, and terribly afraid of the future. I realize now that I was looking too hard for answers, for some assurance that I was making the kinds of decisions that would bring the children and me to a place of safety. Time and again I gave our problem to God, yet I knew it was up to me to act responsibly.

Looking back, I realize I *did* make some basically good decisions. One was to move out of the countryside where we were so isolated, alone—and vulnerable— into a small town to live with an older woman who was a member of our church.

SeventySeven was a study in bluster and verve, constantly letting off steam like the teakettle shape that she was. Somehow, I found favor in her sight, and she insisted that the children and I move in with her. It comforted my spirit greatly to be under her wing. She made all the right clucking noises, as well as wonderfully simple and sumptuous meals. I enjoyed listening to her clatter about in her old-fashioned kitchen and found myself memorizing sounds. It felt like home should have been when I was growing up.

It was a good time in my life. I had no desire for contact with people outside our humble dwelling. SeventySeven talked endlessly about her rich past. It was a welcome relief for me not to have to say much. The few friends I did have were mostly older, and I basked in their quiet stability. With the exception of a younger mother with children close to the ages of my own, I made no effort to associate with anyone my own age.

I preferred to leave the children under the watchful eye of SeventySeven while I stole away to walk the banks of an unpretentious creek not far from the house. There my mind continually turned heavenward as I puzzled over how to pick up the pieces of my life and go on. My existence was overshadowed by the fear that Saintman would return and once again disrupt any plans I might lay. It was like I was checkmated, yet expected to move.

Little did I know that SeventySeven had decided for me what move I needed to make. In her mind, the answer was simple enough: I needed a husband. Someone to protect and provide for the children and me. And she knew just the man.

He worked days as a custodian at a chemical plant and traveled weekends with a small group of gospel musicians. Years ago he had boarded for a time at her home, and they had kept up their friendship through the years. He had never married. She introduced us over the telephone one afternoon. It was quite casual, and I thought nothing much of it.

Little by little, though, she told me all about him, how talented he was, how honest and kind—and what a Wonderful Husband he would make some fortunate woman! Soon W.H. became the inevitable focus of all her conversations with me. I felt my heart warming toward this man whose virtues she daily extolled. The fact that, even though he was forty years her junior, she had fantasized for years about him for herself went over my head like a high-flying bird. She had found a way to vicariously live out her dreams: Me.

There was another fact that was never mentioned, probably because to SeventySeven it didn't matter. Though he worked his job well enough and made wonderful music on the weekends, W.H. was not normal in every way. Some might have called him simple. Others might have blamed it on his "artist's personality." The truth is that he was borderline autistic. It would be some time before I knew this.

So, by the time W.H. and I finally met in person, we had both been programmed quite skillfully by SeventySeven to view each other as very special. I was looking for an answer to my dilemma, and W.H. was looking for someone who could accept him as he was.

We never talked much. I was emotionally bone-dry and, in my present state of mind, his pleasant brain-dryness was overshadowed by his ability to create the most wonderful music! My spirits soared when he played his music and, for a time, that was enough. I didn't want anybody digging around in my mind, anyway.

Naturally, with SeventySeven's persistence and my blissful enjoyment of his music-making, it wasn't long before W.H. decided that he had at long last found his "one and only." He began taking me with him on weekends. It was great fun. I was warmly accepted by his friends and made to feel special and, yes, even beautiful. Best of all, GirlChild loved his big, smiling face.

The day came when W.H. found an opening as night janitor at a high school in a town half the state away. The pay was almost twice what he made locally, and he was anxious to take the job. Would I marry and go with him?

We all thought it was a perfect answer to prayer. Saintman would never find us! God was given joyous credit for providing this sweet escape for the children and me. Why should I question it? And so a date was set.

I was excited but, once again, not so much in love as I thought I was in God's will. My heart was full of gratitude and relief—and W.H.'s wonderful music. However, I still had no understanding at all of what a normal relationship between a man and woman should be. I only knew that I felt very tender for this simple and kindly man. He meant to do only good for me and the children. I accepted this opportunity as my full share, having no concept of life beyond my shattered and sheltered existence. Three years before God had promised to heal me. This must be what He had envisioned!

W.H. and I were married with GirlChild and BoySon as our

attendants. Leaving them in the care of SeventySeven, we left for a honeymoon in Europe. Everything seemed wonderfully happy until our first night together in a hotel. I don't know what I expected, but what happened was beyond imagining. After checking in, we went to our room. W.H.'s big smile seemed frozen on his face. He sat on the bed as we prepared to retire, his eyes glassy. Finally he spoke, very tentatively. He told me that he had no idea how men and women made love. He'd seen fish in an aquarium once…

As he continued talking, I realized with horror that not only was this man totally ignorant of nuptial realities—he was utterly incapable of responding in a normal manner. Shaken and not at all sure what all this was going to mean in the long run, I comforted him with small talk. In a little while we tucked in like two very good children, said our prayers, and turned out the light. We didn't touch. We went to sleep.

Morning came, with W.H. jubilant and ready for a day of touring. Neither of us mentioned the night before. We just got dressed and went to breakfast. Still in shock, I kept telling myself that surely time would take care of everything. But time could never undo the gentle tragedy that nature had worked upon W.H. In most ways he was more a child than an adult. Innocence ruled his being. He always meant well, but he was woefully inept at even the simplest tasks.

Now that I was around him daily, I noticed how he continually repeated words and sentences half aloud to himself, sometimes mixed with other indistinguishable sounds. When especially nervous, he spun objects in his fingers. He had broken both his little fingers as a child by spinning things.

The saddest thing about W.H. was that he was almost normal—almost a man. I made an immediate decision: I would live with him. Whatever it took, I would stick it out. Not only did I not want to hurt him, I was too embarrassed to admit that I'd made a mistake. I could not face being caught, as I thought, out of God's will—not after all I'd been through. It was easier to be noble.

When we got back, GirlChild and BoySon were eager to begin family life. It turned out that BoySon and W.H. became immediate friends. Both were about the same age developmentally, matching BoySon's five years. GirlChild, who always was ready to excuse the wrongs of others, simply accepted her larger playmate. Even so, she had long wanted a father and claimed W.H. wholeheartedly. What did she know of fathers, anyway?

I now had the equivalent of three children, and the burden of keeping everybody going fell to me. At least one was a wage earner! For several months we managed to move forward uneventfully in this dream of half reality. However, as the children matured W.H. fell behind. GirlChild made excuses for him. BoySon, though loving, grew increasingly disconcerted by W.H.'s erratic behavior.

Still, I could not face the situation squarely. I thought it was my place to "have faith and endure," to mediate peace and provide stability. I did not realize how unfair it was being to us all. W.H.'s anxiety ballooned.

"You need to get a better man," he told me gravely. "A man who can do the job."

Dear W.H.—in his own limited way, he was more honest in his evaluation than was I!

As he worsened, life became close to intolerable. Once, when he was trying to do the dishes he couldn't manage to get them clean. After I showed him how, he began taking all the clean dishes out of the cupboard.

"Why are you doing that?" I asked.

"I'm going to do it right! I'm going to do it right!" he said repeatedly, with guileless simplicity.

As time progressed and the harder W.H. tried to "do things right," the more frustrated he became. Realizing there was a discrepancy between who he was and what he thought he ought to be, he felt guilty about it and begged me to punish him. At times he brought me a hairbrush and asked that I spank him. When I refused, he slapped his face or hit his head against a wall, pleading for me to discipline him.

There were occasions when, after we stopped at a red light, he jumped out and ran around our car. Later, contrite and scared, he asked me if I was going to leave him. His vulnerability broke my heart.

I finally sought counseling. After meeting with the two of us, my counselor gave it to me straight. He told me that I was being cruel to W.H. by continuing to submit him to stress that he obviously could never handle. Not only that, I was sentencing my children to an abnormal life if I allowed W.H. to "father" them.

Then he explained W.H.'s problem and, for the first time in my life, I learned about autism.

Stunned, I stammered out to the counselor my moral obligation before God. I could not leave W.H. because he had not committed adultery.

More bluntly than ever my counselor, who was also a Christian, pointed out that not only had W.H. committed no adultery—he had not even committed marriage! My moral obligation fell in the realm of rectifying gross misjudgment. He urged me to take decisive action immediately, before even more unthinkable situations occurred.

I cried so hard on the way home that I could barely see enough to drive. Though impaired, W.H. was guilty of nothing. His spirit was flawless. Of such surely were the angels! I loved him—not the love of a woman for a man, but it was unmistakably love just the same. I did not call an attorney when I got home. I called a minister and asked that W.H be anointed.

The night before Minister arrived, I beseeched God for His healing mercy, wailing aloud and prostrating myself on the floor. It was no artificial demonstration. I would gladly have died if my death could bring healing to W.H. How much subconscious desire was in me to avoid having to deal with the real problem, I do not know. There must have been some, somewhere, but I had no consciousness of it at the time.

I briefed W.H. on what was going to happen, and the next morning he awoke buoyant with excitement. In His simple way,

He trusted God implicitly and looked forward to the experience. His faith charged me with hope.

In due time Minister arrived along with one of W.H.'s loyal friends from his gospel group. We closeted ourselves in a small room and began. W.H. was wearing his largest grin as we knelt in a circle around him. He kept saying that he'd like to be better. He grinned through the whole process. After it was over, W.H. looked up and said he felt good— really good. Maybe he was getting better. But also, maybe it would take a while.

"Rome wasn't built in a day," he said in childlike profundity.

Yes; that had to be it. Flashing another grin, he stood up and shook hands all around.

Twice.

Chapter Twenty

Weed by Weed

He probably felt he was doing his duty.

Initially, I thought this man of the cloth he had come to offer comfort and encouragement. The tone of his voice conveyed seasoned wisdom. His manner was skillfully solicitous. Almost immediately, however, I felt his disapproval and was plunged into confusion and shame.

Evidently he had learned that I might be leaving W.H. In spite of the anointing, I was slowly beginning to face the reality of what my counselor was telling me. W.H.'s attempts to fulfill the responsibility of being a father and husband had become more pitiful than ever.

I had discussed the possibility of my departure with a few people in the church. Now Man-of-the-Cloth sat in my house facing me off with moral judgment. He reminded me of the sacredness of the marriage vow—that I had pledged before God to be joined to W.H. "for better or for worse." Granted this was for worse, he said, but it would be a sin for me to break up our home.

"What God hath joined together, let no man put asunder!" His eyebrows knit ominously above his unblinking eyes as he spoke the words.

I tried to share with him the circumstances of our marriage, but he brushed aside my sentences like bothersome insects. Placing a hand heavily on my shoulder he said, "You have had a rather checkered past."

Nothing he might have said could have hit me harder. I fell instantly into self-reproach and abasement. I had been conditioned since early childhood to accept guilt, regardless of my own perceptions. Ten years of marriage to Saintman had deepened this response, though I felt that God consistently sought to awaken my sensibilities to a higher level.

I was just too emotionally whipped to do anything but roll over like a subservient animal. After leading me through a series of verbal self-effacements, Man-of-the-cloth offered prayer and left, admonishing me to do what I "knew" was right.

That afternoon, while the children were visiting neighbors, W.H. entered such a terrible season of unrest that I ended up hiding in the bushes outside the house in order to avoid his frenzy. Crouching in the dirt, I listened and watched. He ran repeatedly around and around the yard looking for me. He was muttering to himself and calling me pathetically. It reminded me of the way BoySon was when he was frightened that I might leave him, again, with Saintman.

Embarrassed and frightened, I made up my mind to take the children and leave. My moral obligations would have to be sorted out later. Within the week, the children and I relocated in a small town near the sea.

W.H. cried like an abandoned child, but was also obviously relieved. I made no statement as to permanency because I had no idea, myself, what the months ahead might bring.

It was tough. We were forced to move in with strangers, the parents of friends, until I could get a rental. Houses were scarce with waiting lists of up to two years. Employment was tight too. There were fifty applicants for every opening, and my employment history included less than a year of work in a fabric store, about a year at the health-food store and bakery immediately after Saintman and I were married, and five or six months at Mrs. Salad's bank.

We had been there a month when I got a call from a man at a large company located on the outskirts of town. He told me that, in passing through his company's personnel office, he'd chanced to catch sight of my job application. "For some reason," he had picked it up. Would I come for an interview?

Would I!

Arriving at his office, I discovered I was completely unqualified for the job he was offering me. He was the director of data input for the whole company, and I had never even touched a computer. I told him that I had applied for secretarial work; that if I'd known the exact nature of his opening I wouldn't have wasted his time by coming in.

He smiled and asked if I thought I could learn the system. Taking me into the work area, he introduced me to his staff, then gave me an overview of the job. Green screens blipped rapidly as trained fingers keyed in information. I was intrigued and terrified all at once.

Back in his office, he offered me a position with the company. Reaching for some papers on the corner of his desk, my prospective boss fanned them with his thumb like a stack of cards.

"These are the other applications for the position I'm offering you," he said.

I thanked him, a little overwhelmed that I had been singled out, and promised that I'd do my best to make his choice one he would not regret.

When I got home there was a message for me from a man who owned a small house in town. Calling the number, I was invited to look at the house that evening with the option of renting it. Surprised, I asked how in the world he had known that I needed a rental.

"Word gets around," he said. "And I've heard that you are a good woman. I've got thirty people after this house, but if you want it, it's yours."

I went to see the house. A tiny two-story, it was freshly painted, and the rugs had all been shampooed. There was a bit of a front yard and a bay tree in back. I knew I had found our home.

That night I cried myself to sleep. God was there all along, taking care of me, even when I had thought I was blatantly directing my own fate. He was nudging me to wholeness, in the persons of the family in whose home I had found shelter, in my future boss, and in my kindly landlord.

I was on new turf. The people I would now be associating with were Christians all, but without rigidity or religiosity. It would still take time for me to adjust my reference points accordingly, but fresh air was blowing through the windows of my soul. I would never again be the same. This ghetto child of emotional poverty was facing east, as it were, to the rising of understanding.

How tenderly my Father must have looked upon me! For though I was indeed catching the winds of promise in my heart, my mind had been fettered so long by misapprehensions of Him that even now it was impossible that I could walk unscathed into the future. I still had much to overcome!

Yet, I had come so far that my prayers were like rainbows in the night. I was full of hope, full of freshness. I had had an unexpected rendezvous with God through these people, and I wanted to linger in this miracle of peace. I felt insulated by His loving interest in me and, for the time being, did not want to think about anything else.

I did well at my job. After three months I was promoted to supervisor. My boss invested his confidence in me, and I gave him my best. I asked permission to learn more about the system we were using. Soon I was able to initiate ways to improve overall productivity.

I was getting a real sense of my potential capabilities and it felt good. It occurred to me that there were probably many people who, like myself, thought they were inadequate and incompetent when, in fact, they had stores of capabilities. God leaves none of us empty-handed.

Then W. H: started calling and I knew I had unfinished business to tend to.

I had become friends with a local pastor and his wife, whose children were close to the ages of GirlChild and BoySon. A true shepherd, he was genuinely interested in the lives of those who came under his care. When I explained to him the circumstances of my life, he did not remind me of my checkered past. He told me I needed to get an annulment.

I wanted so badly to do just that, but just thinking about it made me feel guilty. Man-of-the-Cloth's voice thundered in my heart. It was familiar battleground, this "sanctified reasoning" that quoted so many Scripture verses and made me feel like a sinner. I was not yet grounded in the knowledge that anyone can amass an arsenal from the sacred canon. Only a prudent hearer of the Word divides it wisely.

I call it the John 21 principle. In verse 22 Jesus told His disciple Peter, "If I want [John] to remain alive until I return, what is that to you? You must follow me" (NIV). The next verse points out that, because of this statement, a rumor spread among the believers that John would not die. But they were incorrect. They had missed the point of what Jesus was saying because they focused on His precise words instead of His intent.

Perhaps my horror of reentering the court system finally tipped the scales. At any rate, I was unable to carry through and finalize my separation from W.H. I comforted myself with the thought that I was submitting to God's will while, in fact, I was only prolonging the inevitable. I gave in to W.H.'s pleading and told him he could come to live with us. It lasted eight months.

Dear W.H. tried hard to be "good." He tried to be a father to the children, but it was a disaster. GirlChild had entered school and was daily exposed to the rudiments of logic. W.H.'s actions often bordered on bizarre.

BoySon felt increasingly disconcerted by W.H.'s repetitious language and inability to understand what BoySon was saying. He had outgrown his large friend.

I realized that I wasn't being fair to anybody, and that something had to be done. It was time I faced myself squarely. Still, I didn't want another marriage to end in failure. It would be like admitting to scandal. Besides, W.H. was innocent. How could I hurt him? I felt like I was standing on the edge of a huge abyss with total, endless darkness below and before me.

"How can you *continue* to hurt him?" Shepherd was firm in his appraisal. "He cannot make the necessary choice. You must, for him and for the sake of your children."

As I cried out my shame and despair Shepherd gently began to probe my picture of God. As we talked, it became painfully obvious to him, and eventually to me, that there was something terribly mixed up in my thinking about God. I also began to see that my self-image was severely damaged.

I was like a neglected garden where weeds had grown wild for years. Though faith and truth had been planted, the weeds kept choking them and stunting their growth. Harsh winds blew mercilessly over the parched ground. Shepherd now entered my garden and began digging out the weeds one by one so faith and truth could thrive and bloom. It was a commitment. He and his family were there to stay.

How I wish that I could write a happy ending to my story right here! How I wish I could tell you that from this time forward my life was okay, that it turned out "happily ever after"! It would fit much more comfortably into our Christian notion of how stories like this are supposed to end.

But, as so many of the stories in the Bible reveal, humanity moves much more slowly toward restoration than we expect. We equate God's power with speed—in earthly terms. We aren't entirely wrong, but often we fail to think in terms of eternity.

Someday, when we step into forever, this earth's history as we know it will shrink into a mere moment. Individual lifetimes will seem but sparks that ignited into immortality, or flashed briefly and were no more. We cannot evaluate the miracle of God's leading in our lives by finite estimation.

My heart was willing, but my humanity was weak. I know now that I never came under the condemnation of heaven. Shepherd worked, weed by weed, to bring my garden to its potential vibrancy—but there were so many weeds! It was a long-range endeavor.

Eight more years of faltering lay ahead of me. It was a good thing I didn't know.

Chapter Twenty-one

A Man of Ashes

After the annulment I did not want to keep W.H.'s name, nor did I want Saintman's back. My maiden name brought me no comfort either, so I took to myself my dear Grandmother Nonnie's maiden name. It made me feel good. She seemed more family to me in her death than did my own mother—and Nonnie I had known very little.

Mom never enjoyed having my children in her home. At one point she told me that, though I was more than welcome to visit, she'd rather I left the children behind. Their innocent exuberance made her nervous. She was as negative about them as she had always been about the rest of the family. It hurt me greatly, but I complied though I hid her feelings from my children.

One morning, while taking a shower, a sudden melancholy gripped my whole being. Why had I been denied so much? Was I forever hobbled to my past? Even as the water spilled over my head I felt as if I had been spilled, without honor, into life.

Suddenly a Bible text came to mind: "I will restore to you the years that the locust hath eaten" (Joel 2:25).

"What?" I said out loud as if someone had spoken to me. Involuntarily, the text again sounded in my mind.

Father, are these words from you? But how could you ever make up to me all the years of emptiness? I'm thirty-two. I cannot go backward. My mother has isolated herself from me. My father...

I couldn't finish my prayer; it hurt too much. As I dried off, I pondered what had just happened. I felt strongly that my heavenly Father was speaking to me directly. Fleeting as it was, I counted this communication as most wonderful.

My precious Father, I hear you so clearly. I don't exactly understand what you are telling me, but it almost doesn't matter. Your presence fills my heart. I love you.

Later that night I got to thinking about my biological father. He had died several years before. My mother didn't tell me for several weeks after the fact. She only told me when she heard through the grapevine that, had I gone to his funeral, I would have come into a small inheritance. If I didn't attend, I could claim only one dollar. She was afraid I'd hear about this from somebody else, so decided to tell me herself.

I was angry with her, not because I wanted the money, but because I should be allowed to make my own decisions. When she implied that she had done me a favor, I balked. At this she acted very insulted, stating that she was shocked to think I might have even considered going. I dropped the subject. Years before I learned it was the best way to handle her when she was upset.

When I had the chance, however, I made my way to the place where he had been laid to rest. Cremated, his ashes were placed in an Elks Club memorial wall in a large cemetery. As I stared at his name, a great emptiness swept over me. I felt as though I had come to the point where I was supposed to tie in to life and the rope had been left dangling.

I traced the date of his birth with my fingers. For a moment my hand was suspended in midair. Then slowly I touched the date of his death. As I took my hand away, something inside of me closed.

My father returned to Switzerland by himself to visit relatives many times when I was little. Evidently he sent my brother and me a little record he made of his voice. My mother never played it for us. Only after I was in high school did I discover it, hidden away among some things in a box. I took it out and played it. His voice sounded far away—a lifetime away. He called me by my nickname and said that he missed his little girl. He used the word Daddy.

Mom was furious when she found out I had played the record. She broke it in two, telling me I was a silly little ninny because I was crying. I was ashamed at the time that his voice had such an effect on me. Now I was crying because he was dead. Why? I had been terrified of him.

There was no resolution in my feelings or thinking that day at the cemetery. Now, as I lay in my bed, the part of me that had closed began to open. One father against another—a man of ashes against the living God.

Oh my Father. No wonder it has taken me so long to think properly about you! It's almost as if my mind and heart have occupied opposite ends of the universe. With my mind I have eagerly reached for you, but my guts have been interred in a cemetery wall!

Teach me to know you! Restore to me the years that the locust has eaten—all the years my heart has been eaten away by hurt and confusion. So much is locked up somewhere, far away from my consciousness. Go there, Father, and make me whole.

My heart throbbed as I prayed. This world must yield its captive to the living God.

More than this, stretch me and make me more than I might have been had all gone well in my life. I want to make up to YOU the years the locust has eaten. Let me be for you a great delight in this world so filled with darkness and sorrow. Yet keep it from me. Father. Do not let me know lest praise spoil my heart. Do it, Father! I want my life and all that you will make of me to be a most wonderful anthem in the courts of heaven.

Shortly after this, a group of Christians who were forming a clinic asked me if I would work for them. They wanted the clinic to have wide visibility and they wanted me to handle public relations. After considering the matter prayerfully I decided to accept the offer.

Days and weeks passed. My job was challenging and I was being paid to learn—and learn I did! Soon I became the head of my department with several staff members under me. With my position came an invitation to sit in on departmental councils. Several times different administrators told me they'd rather see the department lose nearly all its staff rather than lose me. This surprised me because I didn't see myself that way at all. Slowly, however, I began to feel comfortable with their compliments. It gave me the security I needed to excel.

One night I went out under the stars and told God how I felt.

Thank you, Father, for giving me a chance to work in such a motivating atmosphere. I love the demands made upon me. I love coming to grips with complexity and moving on to achievement. I know I'm changing. It excites me a great deal, and frightens me only a little now.

The wind was rustling the tops of the trees, making the warm night air swirl gently around me. How I wished I could join the heavenly choir as they made celestial rafters ring with joyous praise for the great and living God, my Father.

Oh my Father, I desire a special favor from you. Could you put me on heaven's "speaker system," just for a moment?

My heart was pounding. I held my breath, then mentally faced the angelic host. A moment later I lowered my head. A deep shyness made my face warm at the thought of actually communicating with sinless beings. Perhaps I was foolish beyond measure, but my desire was greater than my humility. Addressing all of heaven, I made my request to the angels.

"I am sorry I am a sinful being! The Father deserves the choicest praise and I cannot give it. I know that your greatest delight is singing praises to Him, and I would like you to praise Him now with a new song—a song from a captive of this dreary world. Since I cannot sing in His presence as you can, please, if you will, lift your voices in fullest rapture to Him for me. Tell Him how much I love Him—and that I trust Him!"

In my heart I imagined the happiness of these beings of light as they set about to do what they loved to do best, glad that I'd given them such an opportunity.

The days of summer were passing quickly. With them came

an unexpected situation. Men were finding me attractive. For some reason this possibility had never occurred to me. I found it more curious than pleasant, though pleasant it was. I took none of it seriously.

One young man who attended my church was a college student all of twenty-five years of age. I considered him thoughtful when he started offering to take the children for walks in the evening. He obviously liked children. He always invited me to go along, which I gladly did because I loved being outside. After we got back we usually drank orange juice on my front porch and talked. It dawned on me after a couple of weeks that he probably liked me even more than he liked my children!

Without really deciding, in time I became his "girl"—at least as far as people at the church were concerned. We had many good times and, though he was seven years my junior, it didn't seem to matter. Most of the church members thought I was younger than he was. His mother liked me. My children were happy. Why not?

Then he proposed!

For this I was unprepared. Though I had begun to care about him, things had not come together enough inside of me to make that kind of commitment. Though everyone said we made a handsome couple, I was not sure that we really matched. His world was still collegiate. Something inside of me was at least one hundred and ten.

His mother found out about my "past" and her attitude toward me changed drastically. My spirits took a plunge. I told TwentyFive that I could not marry him. He didn't take it well. Sometimes he drove away from my house squealing his tires.

Other men made known their interest in me. My initial feelings of intrigue deteriorated into panic when I heard one or two church members were circulating unkind remarks about all the men who were lining up at my doorstep. Though I had never behaved in an unseemly manner and had only dated TwentyFive, I was greatly dismayed. The words "checkered past" haunted me and I began to feel a nameless guilt.

About this time there came to my door a gentleman of dignified demeanor whom I did not know. I'd seen him at church, but had no idea who he was or what he was now doing at my house. I greeted him through a closed screen and waited for him to make clear the purpose of his visit.

Screendoor made small talk at first, then mentioned that he'd heard a lot about me, especially that I was a beautiful woman. I was dumbstruck and said nothing. I just stared at him. Thinking back, I don't remember all that Screendoor said except that he ended up telling me that I needed to be careful. My face was burning when I shut the door.

What was happening? Did people assume that I was wanton merely because I was divorced and living alone—and men found me attractive? Self-doubt began creeping into my mind again. Was I guilty and didn't know it? Surely a dignified person like Screendoor must know what he was talking about. Like SeventySeven, I decided that the answer was simple enough: I needed to be married. Then people would stop talking. Then maybe they'd leave me alone.

I hadn't been at the clinic long when another man joined the staff. Everyone seemed to know him and told me what a nice guy he was. Guy kept to himself even at the church we both attended, so I was surprised when he started talking to me at work. He offered to let me borrow a religious book he thought I'd enjoy, then his records. Before long, he was lending me his time.

Though I wasn't extremely attracted to Guy, he was certainly more my age than TwentyFive. Still, our friendship developed more because I didn't resist than because I felt anything for him. He was nice and made no physical advances on me whatsoever. If our relationship was bland, it was at least safe.

When TwentyFive learned about my growing friendship with Guy, he pressured me to reconsider marriage with him. Finally, fired by TwentyFive's persistence, Guy also proposed. Foolishly, I thought I had to make a choice between the two of them. And I had additional incentive to get married. I discovered that Saintman had moved to a town about four hours away!

Though I favored Twenty-five, I felt Guy was a more appropriate choice and was sure I could learn to love him. When the people at the clinic learned about our engagement, they were ecstatic. Their enthusiasm seemed to confirm that I was doing the right thing.

It was Cinderella time all over again. Someone offered to sew my dress, another offered to see to the wedding flowers, and still another volunteered to undertake the reception.

I was off one hook all right—and caught on the point of another!

Chapter Twenty-two

Ceramics

Shepherd looked worried when I asked him to perform the ceremony.

"You aren't acting like a bride-to-be," he said.

I was sitting in his office. It was just a few weeks until the wedding, and it was true that I was not filled with joy. Guy and I were running into a real problem: communication—or rather, the lack of it. Whenever something came up that needed discussion, Guy said, "Don't worry about it." Period. End of discussion.

I did not tell Shepherd about this. Instead, I convinced him that everything was okay; that I was just a little overwhelmed with all the preparations being made. Gentleman that he was, he accepted my word. I wish he hadn't.

Perhaps I thought I had experienced so much disaster that I was immune to anything bad. I *was* experiencing a heightened sense of rationality, and was functioning well in the normal scope of my employment. The children were pleased at the thought of finally being a "complete" family. God had promised to make up to me the years of emptiness. How could anything be seriously wrong?

Had I examined my prayer life, I might have seen where I was going. I did not ask God for guidance; I only asked Him to stay close to me, and this I felt He did. Misinterpreting closeness for sanction, I ignored all the red flags in my relationship with Guy.

Instead, I allowed my growing fear of Saintman's proximity to catapult me into the safety of matrimony. I set my face to the wind and told none of these things to anyone.

A couple of weeks before the ceremony I was summoned to Shepherd's office. When I got there he was on the phone. Waving me to silence, he motioned me to carefully pick up the phone on his secretary's desk. I held down the button as I lifted the receiver, then slowly released it. In an instant I recognized the voice at the other end of the line. It was Saintman! He was telling Shepherd about himself, in the third person.

Shepherd raised his eyebrows and put his hand over the receiver. "Is this Saintman?"

I nodded. I heard Saintman tell Shepherd that he was a "godly" man and that I had deserted him to run off with another man. He urged that my future husband be warned not to marry me.

When Shepherd asked who he was, Saintman told him that it did not matter. What mattered was that a wicked woman should not be allowed to continue her hypocrisy. When Shepherd pressed him, he hung up.

Shaken to the core of my being, I could not be comforted. Though I finally pulled myself together enough to leave Shepherd's office, I was in no way coherent. Any hope that I might come to my senses about marrying Guy was lost that day.

Guy and I were married. We left for our honeymoon with roses decorating our car. Begging off lovemaking that first night because he had a cold, consummation of our vows waited until the following day. The experience was marked by eagerness— Guy hurried to get it over with. He seemed not to want to touch me. I felt hurt and wondered why he was so passionless, but decided he must be nervous. So passed our first week as husband and wife.

We returned home and took up our jobs at the clinic. Girl-Child, determined to make a father out of Guy, tried to evoke his interest in her. He was pleasant, but remained distant. I remember her climbing up into his lap one evening. She tried to cuddle into arms that did not fold around her. After a while she silently climbed down and went to her bedroom. Later I spoke to Guy about it, but all he said was, "Don't worry about it."

Soon our family life settled into a silent standoff. I defended Guy to the children, thereby cutting them off from talking to me about their feelings. In due time his indifference toward them turned into harshness, and GirlChild bore the brunt of it.

Unexpectedly, I got pregnant in our third month of marriage. For a while the prospect of a new baby made everyone happier. GirlChild was ecstatic. She was halfway through her eleventh year and more than eager to help mother a baby. For me it marked the end of the Saintman era—a child of mine was not his!

With my pregnancy, Guy's lack of interest in me accelerated. He had never wanted to touch me; now I felt abandoned. I didn't know what to think and was too embarrassed to speak about it to anyone. People who knew us thought we were happy because that's how we appeared on the outside. I was back to one-word prayers: *Father...*

Sure I had used up my share of mercy and compassion, I could only utter God's name. Going to woods nearby, I stretched full length in the leaves and sobbed out my sorrow. I was reaping what I had sown. We would have to make the best of it.

Youngest was born on Easter. A beautiful little girl with wonder in her eyes, she captured my heart from the start. When we came home from the hospital, GirlChild's exuberance vanished, and she ignored her little sister almost entirely. I understood why. The last time a baby entered her life she was demoted, not to second place, but to no place at all. And now Guy's sudden awakening of feelings were not directed toward her, but toward his own offspring. It must have felt awful to GirlChild to see a man she could not evoke to love, loving this little stranger.

In time, GirlChild's natural instincts took over, and she mothered Youngest with unfaltering devotion. Nevertheless, on the inside damage was being done that would be exhibited a few years later as intense self-destruction. For now it took the form of sulking disobedience. Guy reacted swiftly and with alarming physical harshness.

Caught in the middle, I didn't know how to react. Whenever I tried to protect GirlChild, Guy became even meaner. If I offered no interference, GirlChild was left to pitiless discipline and the knowledge that I had not defended her. Confused, I was not consistent.

On more than one occasion, Guy subdued GirlChild by partially suffocating her. Placing his hand over her nose and mouth and bending one arm behind her back, he held her until she went limp. During those times her eyes were wild with terror. Sometimes he threw her against things. I pleaded with him on her behalf, but to no avail. Afterward she spoke to no one. Guy thought he had succeeded. I knew GirlChild better. I also knew I had to act.

The next time it happened I attacked Guy from behind, knocking him loose from GirlChild. He turned on me pushing me to the floor and striking me in the face, giving me a black eye. GirlChild flew at him.

"Leave my Mommy alone!" she screamed.

When he went for her, I went for him. It became an animal brawl. However, it shook Guy up. He avoided conflict for a time after that. I went to see a counselor.

It was hard for me to face counseling. This was my third marriage, and I feared the counselor would assume from the beginning that the problem was solely with me. The members at church were beginning to notice that not all was well in our home. It came back to me that someone said I went through men like some women went through clothes. Sick with humiliation I nevertheless continued with the counselor for GirlChild's sake.

Guy eventually agreed to go with me, but he only went to a few sessions. Exposure of his actions seemed to help, though. There were no more smotherings. However, he remained uncommunicative, and most of the time he went around with anger in his eyes. I finally quit going because it seemed futile to go alone. Guy and I were no closer to an answer.

My prayers were expanding. Little by little Shepherd, who knew by now what was happening, convinced me that I had not used up my share of God's compassion. Accepting this open door, I ran toward it. Sitting under a tree one evening watching the sun turn the sky into an artist's canvas, I prayed.

Father, I'm so ashamed! How could I have gotten us into such a mess so quickly! I know I missed a turn somewhere, but what matters now is that GirlChild is suffering badly, and it's my fault! Please, for her sake, help us! BoySon suffers, too, under Guy's cutting remarks and hard manner. What have I done? What have I done to my children!

For a while all I could do was weep. I remonstrated with myself before the Lord for my unlikeness to Him.

How can you possibly still want me to live for you? I feel utterly disqualified! Sure, some Christians have been divorced, but look at me! My life looks like I should be living in Hollywood. I hate it! You know I never wanted even one marriage to fail, and now this one is failing too. What am I to do? Father, I am so sorry! I never meant for this to happen! I need you. Please help me. Please speak to me—anything! I desperately need to hear your voice!

Very distinctly, there came to my mind a single word: Ceramics.

Since I was taking a class in ceramics, I thought my mind had wandered. A hot flush of embarrassment shot through me. I ought to keep my mind on my prayers! Shaking my head to clear my thinking, I apologized and again asked God to speak to me.

The word came more forcefully than before: Ceramics. A sudden thrill took my breath away. I knew I had not thought this word by myself.

Ceramics, Father? Why ceramics? What are you trying to tell me?

I began to consider the process of making ceramics. First comes a mold. I needed to be molded into God's likeness.

A pudding like "slip" is poured into the mold, where it hardens into "green ware." Extremely delicate, green ware is easily broken, but may be softened again and re-poured. This can be done as often as necessary. Yes, I have crumbled many times.

Though delicate, green ware must be smoothed with a sharp scalpel before it is fired into its fixed form. I put my hands over my face and wept.

During the first firing, green ware is placed into an extremely hot kiln and baked, rendering it stronger. Once hardened, it can be handled with less chance of breakage. Saintman!

Firing also exposes more defects. These must be sandpapered away, so the surface can be smooth and ready for coloring. W.H.—*Father, I'm listening!*

I remembered how hard it was for my instructor to convince me to apply hideous gray, lumpy paint to my hardened, smoothed dinnerware

"This can't be right," I said. "How can this ugly mixture ever produce the color I want?"

"Trust me," she said.

She was right. The ugly gray paint turned into a beautiful color when fired. Jumping up I began to run. Down a gravel road and through a field I flew, laughing. I would trust Him! God was going to take my ugly gray lumps of failure and fire them into wonderful colors! I began to call out to Him.

I hate it, but I love it! Oh Father, let the colors be beautiful. Make them like the colors of the rainbow. Make them so vivid that everyone who sees them will praise your name. Make them so warm that they will love you forever. I want to be beautiful for you, Father. Make me intelligent, compassionate, and wise. Let the whole universe shout with joy that in the weakest of the weak you are strong. Make yourself beautiful in me!

Spontaneously I began to sing my prayer, a melody born of love and gratefulness to the living God, out of a heart free in its abandonment, for His marvelous redemption.

Chapter Twenty-three

CalfEyes

When I first met Guy he was in the company of a rather strange, calf-eyed man who walked as if there were sponges in his shoes. CalfEyes worked at the clinic, though I never got to know him. The staff at the clinic was a warm-hearted bunch, so he was accepted in spite of his strangeness. When CalfEyes left to move to another state, he and Guy corresponded faithfully.

After Guy and I married, I happened to run across one of CalfEyes' letters. Declaring deep devotion to Guy, he had sent along some money. When I questioned Guy, he mumbled that he had sent the money back.

On our second wedding anniversary, Guy and I took an extended trip. How I hoped it would bring healing to our relationship. We camped in the high mountains where the heavens were cut into shape by rocky peaks. Misty clouds brooded and fought in windy masses, sprayed us with moisture, then parted to reveal a penetratingly blue sky. I was enthralled.

At night I lay in the dark, listening to the comforting stirrings of campground life mixed with the rustle and voice of woodland creatures. And I waited. Waited for Guy to talk to me. Waited for him to draw me close and make our splintered existence whole.

Guy lay on his back, arms at his sides, unmoving except for the rise and fall of his chest. Snuggling up close, I wrapped my arms around his arm and put my face against his shoulder.

Though he did not actually repel me, in no way did he acknowledge my presence.

I whispered in his ear: "Please talk to me, Guy. Please don't shut me out!"

He stared straight up, saying nothing. I could stand it no longer and started to cry. During our entire trip Guy never responded. By the time we returned home, I was devastated. Guy looked robust.

Several months later I got very sick. My spirit was so low I didn't have the fight in me to get well. One day after church a lady doctor who was a widow came up to me in the ladies' room and asked how I was doing. I could tell from the tone of her voice and the expression on her face that she meant her question to be more than a casual, "How are you today?" We were alone at the time, and her obvious concern for my well-being unleashed my emotions. I threw myself into her arms and began sobbing uncontrollably. It took me several minutes to calm down. I was thankful no one else walked in.

Puzzled, LadyDoc asked what was wrong. I blurted out that I didn't know why my husband couldn't love me, why he wasn't attracted to me. I told her that I could step out of the shower in his presence and he wouldn't even look up. I couldn't stand my own reflection in the mirror. What was wrong with me?

"Wait a minute!" LadyDoc interrupted. "We need to talk!"

And so we did. She came to see me at times when we could be alone in the house, and little by little she drew the story out of me. She urged us to seek more extensive professional help. Somehow the thought that there might be help for us was enough for me. My illness left me exhausted, and I may have fallen asleep before she left. In any case, I began to improve after that.

BoySon wasn't faring well under Guy's harshness. It was true that he wasn't the most industrious worker at the ripe old age of eight, but he was sweet tempered and very anxious to please. Unfortunately, BoySon also moved rather slowly, which Guy interpreted as studied laziness. He often accosted the boy verbally, belittling him until his little face would freeze with despair. It was not a teacher-student relationship. It was animal trainer and beast, and a poor trainer at that.

I dared not interfere, because that only made Guy angry and more abrasive. Sometimes I tried talking it through with him later, but he either ignored me entirely or yelled about how worthless BoySon was. There was so much pent-up violence in Guy. It made my stomach turn.

One afternoon I found BoySon lying on his bed, staring at the ceiling. I sat down next to him and tousled his hair. He continued staring at the ceiling. I touched his arm, then leaned directly over his face until I engaged his eyes.

"BoySon, I love you. I'm sorry that life has been so hard for you, but do not copy the men that have made you so miserable. True manhood is as gentle as it is strong. None of the men who have been in our lives have expressed true manhood. I know it's a big order for you but, in spite of the wrong examples you've been exposed to, I want you to learn true manhood. God will show you how. I know He's as unhappy with the way things have turned out as you are."

BoySon's eyes never left mine as I spoke. They filled with tears, which spilled silently over the sides.

"It's okay to cry," I reassured him. "Brave men cry; then they get up and fight. I want you to fight, BoySon, but not with your fists or with a mean tongue. I want you to fight with your heart."

I could see the pain in my little son, the despair. I took him in my arms, rocked him, and let him cry.

"I'm so proud of you," I said. "You are a fine son. I need you."

GirlChild, ever buoyant and running headlong into life, wanted so much for everything to be all right. But I could see changes in her. She was becoming more selfish. I sensed this was an attempt to make up to herself for the cruel and unfair treatment she received at Guy's hand. She began retreating into her own private little world.

At the time I didn't know how to deal adequately with her,

but I recognized what was happening and reassured her in every way I could that I loved her, that she was special. Reminding her that she was my firstborn, I told her that no one could ever take that place away from her. I complimented her on her ability to play the piano and on her talent in communicating with people. She was very worldly-wise for one so young and was beginning to experience God.

GirlChild desperately wanted my love, but at the same time she became more hateful toward me. I understood why: I had done this to her. Unintentionally, I had brought GirlChild grief far too overwhelming for her to sort out properly at such a tender age. She needed to lash out at somebody, and I was safe. I would never stop loving her.

She needed to test me—to test the strength of my commitment to her. She needed solidarity in her life. In time, she would bring us both to the brink of human endurance. What we were experiencing now was only the beginning.

Shortly after Guy and I returned from our vacation we changed to another counselor—a woman who was a Christian. During the first session, Guy got up from his chair and began pacing the room.

"I don't know what's wrong!" he said.

His fists were doubled tightly, and he looked menacing. Counselor sat poised, but far back in her chair and absolutely still. Later, she confided in me that she was afraid Guy was going to hit her. She was probing deeply. What had Guy felt on our wedding night? Was it really a cold that prevented him from consummating our vows?

Guy didn't answer her. When she asked him if he had had other sexual experiences with women, he admitted to two brief encounters. When asked how the women responded, Guy said they didn't like it that he didn't talk to them.

As I listened to Counselor draw Guy out I watched his thinly veiled fury. A strange peace came over me. So I wasn't the only one. This was a long-standing pattern with him. Guy had a hard time relating to *all* women. I learned that his father had often beaten his older brother with a two-by-four and that his mother was so domineering that his father finally left her for another woman.

What did this mean for us? When the session was over, Counselor suggested to Guy that he seek a male counselor. He agreed to do so.

One evening Guy told me that his counselor had given him a test and that his graph lines had nearly gone off the paper. I called my counselor and asked her what that might mean.

Incredulously, she asked, "You mean he told you? It means that he scored very, very badly."

I told her I didn't think he understood this. She only replied that it was going to take a lot of counseling, maybe years of it, to help Guy work through his problems. She said that while she was not suggesting that I leave him, she would certainly understand if I decided it was best for the children that we not continue to live with him.

That night I waited until everyone was asleep, then slipped outside. Sitting down at the edge of a field, I thought about the circumstances of my life and the possibility of leaving Guy. Recently, I had read a text from the book of Jeremiah: "These are the words of the Lord to Zion: Your injury is past healing, cruel was the blow you suffered. There can be no remedy for your sore, the new skin cannot grow" (Jeremiah 30-12 13 NEB).

I felt intense discouragement. Had God joined those who would leave me condemned, abandoned to reap the misery of my choices? Were my children thereby sentenced to physical and mental abuse? Was there no way of escape? Was this justice?

I thought my heart would break. Did it matter that, in a very real sense, life was being slowly crushed out of us? Momentarily I flushed with a thought: "If this is the case, I want no part of God!"

Slamming my hand down on the ground, I denounced such thinking. I chose to believe that God was more than my understanding of him at that moment. I would cry out to Him despite what I was feeling. Had I not learned already that His plans for us far exceed our highest dreams?—even when we miserably and repeatedly fail to reach His standard for our lives?

Going back into the house, I picked up my Bible and opened it to where I had been reading in Jeremiah. Turning the page I read, "I will cause the new skin to grow and heal your wounds, says the Lord, although men call you the Outcast, Zion, nobody's friend" (verse 17).

So! My injury was past healing—there was no human remedy for my sore. No new skin was going to grow naturally. But God was going to cause skin to grow anyway! He would heal me, even though I was an outcast.

I dared to believe. In Him, I would defy life as it came to me. I would allow God's new skin to grow across my scarred heart. I would learn how to live all over again.

Oh my Father, can there be any greater miracle? I am about to walk through a wall. I don't know how you will do it, but it doesn't matter. I cannot lose faith in you now. Please help me to learn how to know you. Beyond a shadow of a doubt, I have come to this life impaired. I have been a mess! I need all the new skin you are willing to give me. Let it grow. Father, and replace what is hopelessly damaged and beyond mending.

I went back outside and let the gentle night hold me softly—as softly as I knew my heavenly Father held me. And why not? Would I not hold any of my children, no matter how errant they were, should they come to me needing comfort, protection, and care? It never mattered to me so much what they did as that they survived the crisis and grew stronger and wiser.

Events would someday be forgotten. My children were priceless. And so, once again, God taught me in spite of myself.

Chapter Twenty-four

He Swept the Skies Aside

Though the situation between Guy and me did not improve, heaven seemed to break open. Light seemed to be pouring through a dark glass.

In passage after passage of Scripture I heard God speaking to me. I read in Isaiah, "Yet the Lord is waiting to show you his favour, yet he yearns to have pity on you; for the Lord is a God of justice. Happy are all who wait for him!

"Weep no more. The Lord will show you favour and answer you when he hears your cry for help. The Lord may give you bread of adversity and water of affliction, but he who teaches you shall no longer be hidden out of sight, but with your own eyes you shall see him always. If you stray from the road to right or left you shall hear with your own ears a voice behind you saying, this is the way; follow it" (Isaiah 30:18-21, NEB).

He who was teaching me was no longer hidden from my sight! At last I had a promise that touched the core of my soul's longings. He would not go away from me, even if I strayed, because He knew I didn't want to stray! I had never wanted to stray! He understood how dismayed I was to find myself so out of line with His will.

Soon after that I dreamed I was standing before two massive doors. They must have been fifteen feet high and ten feet wide. I knew the Father was behind those doors, and I needed entrance to Him. I began pounding the doors with my fists, shouting to

Him with tears. Nearly spent, I closed my eyes, but continued pounding on the door. At last I opened my eyes, only to discover that, in fact, I was beating on His great chest!

When I awoke I quickly slipped out of bed and went outside onto the back deck.

Oh Father, I am so sorry! How foolish I have been. I have known no other language than begging. I have pleaded with you when you needed no pleading. I have yelled to you from this earth as if you were hard of hearing or would not listen if I did not exhaust myself in the process of crying out to you. Once I said I'd crawl to you, but you don't want me to crawl! You are lifting me onto my feet, and so I shall stay. It doesn't matter what other people think of me. I am Yours.

I turned to go back inside. At the door I stopped and looked up into the sky. *I love your warm chest. Father. I love how you deal with me.* Momentarily embarrassed at my own words, my eyes dropped. Impulsively, I whispered, *I think I like you, Father!*

A puff of soft wind brushed against my face ever so lightly. In my heart I heard my Father say, "I like you too."

You do?

I was startled by such a thought. I knew God loved us all. It never occurred to me that He might *like* us. Especially me—His errant, confused daughter who seemed so prone to run blindly into brick walls. With my face lifted heavenward, I beheld the perfection of the galaxies. How could God...?

And I was filled with His smile.

A few weeks later, Guy decided to live with his mother for a few months. We never discussed it, but there was an intuitive understanding between us that it was my decision whether he ever came back to live with us. For now, I was just glad for the break.

Once Guy left, I began to receive visits from well-meaning church members who urged me to make my home a place where my husband would want to dwell, to be satisfied with the man I was married to—as if I had grown tired of him and was seeking to gain the freedom to pursue others! I refused to discuss anything with them. Our family life was not the property of onlookers, even if it meant that some were bound to draw unwarranted conclusions.

Nevertheless, my heart ached for acquittal. It was hard enough to face the results of my own choices without feeling a barrage of judgmental sentiments from others. I was willing to accept the responsibility of having stepped out of God's will, but I hated the suspicion of whoredom. It burned my spirit greatly and made me feel dirty.

How I wished for an earthly father who would put my accusers on the run! I fantasized how he would stand protectively in front of me, saying with all the rage of parental indignation, "Leave her alone! She's *my* daughter. I will not have you saying such things about her!" They would be turned away because of his strength and nobility.

Many nights my tears found their way to my pillow as my insides wrenched and turned. *Father*, I whispered. It wasn't really a prayer. I just needed Him so much.

Often I awoke in the middle of the night praying, sleep having only slightly interrupted my thoughts. My petitions were already in my mouth as consciousness dawned. Eventually I fell back to sleep. When I awoke in the morning I knew that these times in the night could never be shared casually with another human being. It was too private, too honest, too sacred.

One night I awoke in this fashion and began gathering my prayer-thoughts, hungering for reassurance that God understood my heart. I longed to bring Him pleasure, but felt I only brought Him reproach because of my pitiful passage through this world. I needed to know that He knew I had not deliberately disobeyed or forsaken Him. Though I felt I had no right to ask, I wished for release from the awful circumstances the children and I were in. And so I made my petition until I dropped back to sleep.

I awoke very early the next morning, turned over, and picked up my Bible. Opening to Psalm 18, I began to read. What I found there left me stunned. Here was the Father for whom I so longed! He heard me in my distress and rose to my defense. His nostrils smoking. He swept the skies aside as He descended to rescue me. Then He brought me to an open place—a place where I was not condemned. I was free to grow in Him. He declared His delight in me! If I had read no more, this alone would have filled me. But the passage continued: "In his sight I was blameless and kept myself from willful sin" (Psalm 18:23, NEB).

My Father knew that I never meant to sin, that I had been trying all along to follow His will! Holding my Bible close to my chest, it seemed it could scarcely contain my beating heart. For a long time I sat there, very still, and tried to take it all in. Finally, I lowered my Bible and read more.

"Thou, Lord, dost make my lamp burn bright, and my God will lighten my darkness. With thy help I leap over a bank, by God's aid I spring over a wall" (verses 28, 29).

God was my shield. He was setting me secure on the mountain of His strength. By His grace, I would leap over the barriers that kept me from knowing Him, as it was my privilege to know Him. Too overwhelmed to process these things any further, I laid my Bible aside and got up to meet the day.

In spite of the inspiration I received from my Bible when I first woke up, throughout the morning a cloud began to form in my mind. Life had turned too many cruelties upon me. I must not grasp at such marvelous things so quickly. Had not I proven myself a fool many times over? Perhaps I was deluded. And so, slowly, I came to feel I had to "give back" the passage in Psalm 18. I would not count it. I would not claim it as my own.

As soon as I decided to do this, an awful sadness swept over me. Strangely, though, I also felt at peace. That night I again stood under the stars and gave back Psalm 18.

Father, if you really want me to have this passage, please give it to me again. Then I will know that I dare to take it to myself.

Later, sheet to chin, my mind replayed again and again the picture of my Father "sweeping the skies aside"—for me! After trying to go to sleep, I gave up and switched on a light.

In my devotional reading that day, Jeremiah's story of the pot-
ter and the clay had turned up. I opened to it and read, "Now
and then a vessel he was making out of the clay would be spoilt
in his hands, and then he would start again and mould it into
another vessel to his liking" (Jeremiah 18:4, NEB).

The words, "in his hands" jumped out at me! Could I be in
God's hands and yet be spoiled?

Father, have I really been in your hands all along?

Was this His reaffirmation of Psalm 18? I felt comforted, but
not quite ready to believe. As I meditated on these matters, I
decided to move the little red silk marker attached to my Bible
to Jeremiah 18 so as to locate the passage readily in the morning. At that moment the marker was in 2 Samuel. As my fingers
touched it, some words caught my eye. What was this?

"Smoke rose from his nostrils" (2 Samuel 22:9, NEB). My
heart almost stopped beating. "He swept the skies aside as he
descended" (verse 10). It took me a few moments to be sure. It
was Psalm 18, right there, in 2 Samuel 22!

My heart was filled with reverence for God. It was as it I had
been led to the great throne room of heaven where the mighty
God of the universe sat. But I was not taken to the imposing
front entrance where angels stood guard. No, I was shown the
side entrance—the entrance where a child might slip in unno-
ticed to see her father. And so I did, as it were, to His knees. And
there I lay my head in perfect safety.

On the advice of my attorney, I filed for an annulment. Guy
did not contest it. He ignored it—like everything else.

During this time Screendoor took up Guy's cause with a ven-
geance. Writing letters to people I didn't even know, but who
might be influential in whether or not I remained in the good
graces of the church, he set about to ruin me.

GirlChild came out of church one day flushed and terribly agitated. All the way home I could tell that something was wrong,
but she refused to talk about it until we walked through the front
door. Then it was as though a dam had broken loose.

"They can't talk about you like that!" she yelled. "I hate them! If they are Christians, I don't ever want to be one!"

A church member had pulled GirlChild aside and warned her not to grow up like her mother. "They said ugly things about you," she blurted, "but I told them they didn't know what they were talking about. Mommy, tell them what really happened!"

What could I say to GirlChild? I did not want to bring further hurt to Guy's already troubled existence. His abusiveness and confusion were not to be weapons in my hands against him. I understood all too well how damaged a person can be in this life. I would not raise my heel against him nor would I add one weight to his burden.

Simultaneously, I was riddled with remorse so black that I did not know how to deal with it. I did not understand it, nor could I fit it into the fabric of God's weaving. It became so consuming that for several days I had a hard time doing my job. In the evenings I came home exhausted and depressed. I doubted myself in every way. I was not at all certain that God wanted me to end my marriage to Guy, yet neither was I certain He wanted me to stay. I wanted Him to tell me, point-blank, what I should do.

Instead, God told me nothing. It was a time of weaning for me. For too many years I had submitted to barking orders. I needed to become acquainted with a new concept of God's will, one that was far superior than emergency Sinai-ism.

God was carefully cutting my spiritual umbilical cord. Dependence upon Him can be unhealthy if it strips the mind and soul of its independence. God did not want to become another dominator in my life. He wanted to teach me self-government.

Chapter Twenty-five

Like an Eaglet

Old, familiar weaknesses were overtaking my spirit. Though I had learned much about God, feelings of abandonment and loss were winning the day. On the brink of learning the difference between sonship and servanthood, I faltered.

My Father had cradled me in His bosom. He had taken pleasure in me. He had allowed me free entrance into His presence and was patiently, skillfully teaching me that I had value beyond the price of even the most faithful servant. The thought that He might like me had been a revelation. But my earthly birthright was an ugly, low self-esteem, and this now rose inside my heart like a tower of demons.

How dare I consider that I was anything but the most shameful of creatures? How could so much tragedy come to a truly good person? There had to be a reason why I was continually unloved by those who should have loved me most, and that reason must lie in some fault of mine. There were still questions, questions, questions that were based more on remorse than on logic. There were no answers. Old memories surfaced.

One night I dreamed about my sister and awoke grieving for her, or, more correctly, for the relationship with her that had never existed. I wanted so badly to be held!

Why didn't God just clap His mighty hands in heaven and break these emotional chains in my mind? As I look back, I am now satisfied that God was choosing the better part for me, though it would be some time before I understood this. It has everything to do with why it is taking Him so long to bring this wayward world home.

Long ago God could have herded all His earth-bound children into divine holding pens, fattened them in a perfect, sheltered environment and proclaimed to a watching universe His ability to bring order out of chaos. What He would not have had is the intelligent companionship of people who applaud the matchless wisdom of His ways because they understand those ways from personal experience.

We err in our understanding of Scripture when we cite as a blueprint for everyone the emergency methods that God may use on occasion in dealing with a few. It's easy to wish that God would deliver all of us from our troubles the way He delivered the Israelites from the armies of Egypt at the Red Sea: No thought required. The answer is just there. Occasionally God intervenes dramatically in the lives of Christians today as He did with ancient Israel, and it is right that we should treasure these evidences of His leading. But there are lessons we can never learn through that kind of guidance. Obedience is not the highest compliment to God if it is not undergirded by adequate thinking. Slaves are not sons. Or daughters.

I was coming to realize that my problems in adulthood stemmed largely from childhood emotional deprivation, and I longed for God to give *me* a Red Sea deliverance. He wanted more than that for me, and was teaching me that I could obtain relief from circumstances that way, but not maturity.

It was time for me to put away the gnawing self-destruction that continually undermined my best intentions. In His choicest wisdom, my Father knew I must come to grips with my damaged past and leave it behind me forever. He was not holding me to it—nor would He hold it away from me. The choice to be freed from it was mine. He wanted me to be strong enough in my knowledge of Him to become independent.

Independence, not defiance, is the cornerstone of freedom.

Independence allows choice, and those who have come to

know God as He truly is will freely and actively give Him their allegiance. His ways will be lauded as magnificent, His requests will be honored as splendid, and fellowship with Him will be counted as exquisite.

I was like a young eaglet that must be pushed from the safety of the nest in order to learn to soar. And, not unlike an eaglet, the first time out I would plummet straight down. My wings, though made to fly, would flap furiously and quite uselessly in the air as I made my descent. My heavenly Parent would be there to catch me on His great back, but I would be full of squawks and totally exhausted by the ordeal. Only later, when soaring high and free, could I understand His wisdom in not protecting me from falling.

Thus, though filled with the promises of God and warmed by His love, in a fit of grief and panic I lost my bearings. A few people at church treated me harshly because I had obtained an annulment from Guy without what they considered to be adequate scriptural grounds. This hurt caused me to prematurely accept the friendship of a young Christian man in a pinstripe suit, convincing myself that I was safe in doing so since I felt totally unattracted to him.

Most of my contact with Pinstripe was over the telephone, so I was even further comforted that no harm could come of it. However, as my troubles escalated, so did our relationship though we saw each other only sporadically.

As time went on I came to realize that Pinstripe was very eager that our relationship develop into something permanent, and this made me feel good even though I did not share his enthusiasm. His interest in me seemed a miracle after a divorce and two annulments. He was a professional man who owned his own company. Maybe I was okay after all! Still, I hesitated. I did not want to get burned again.

Then it happened. One day the manager of the clinic called me into his office and informed me that, because of my separation from Guy and now my subsequent friendship with Pinstripe, they were going to have to let me go. The clinic was a

Christian (though not church-related) organization, and they could employ only people with the highest of moral qualifications. He hoped this did not put me in too serious a bind.

Too serious a bind? I had been investigating an extremely attractive job possibility at another company six months earlier, which I had an excellent chance of getting. I quit pursuing it because this same man, who was now informing me that I was being fired, had impressed upon my mind how much the clinic needed me. Now I had three weeks to find something else.

For two days I could think of little more than welfare and the rat-infested housing I'd endured when I left Saintman. Devastated, I said nothing to people at the church—not even to Shepherd, who I was avoiding because of my problems with Guy and my new relationship with Pinstripe. However I did tell Pinstripe. He immediately suggested marriage and I agreed.

If I didn't love him, I appreciated his treatment of the children. He tussled with them and they liked him. They had been through enough. I would not subject them to welfare and rats.

Thus it was that Pinstripe and I signed a contract on a wonderful, two-story house in the country, got married, and moved in. Everyone was notified after the fact.

I loved Oak Crest, as I called our five acres. The house reminded me so much of the big house I had grown up in though, in fact, it was much prettier. It had a large front porch, sliding doors between front room and parlor and, most wonderful of all, in the master bedroom was a closet with a high window! I couldn't see anything out of it but the sky, but I loved the sky. Surely God had brought me home.

My happiness over Oak Crest was the crumb from the Master's table that I had longed for. BoySon climbed the tallest oak tree in the back yard and hung a rope swing. GirlChild was ecstatic about her room. It was almost as large as the master bedroom, with windows that let in the sun. It was more than any of us had ever had before.

Youngest had her own room, too. Smaller, its closet was almost like a little second room. She bubbled with pleasure when

I painted her dressers and bookcase white, added lime-green knobs, and bought her a white bedspread with pink flowers and lime-green leaves.

For the first time in years I felt a surge of hope.

This was our homestead. In it the children would grow strong. Eventually they would marry and bring their children home. We would play here, grow here, and love here. We were a family!

Pinstripe, though increasingly domineering and rigid, worked hard on the place. The first year we planted thirty fruit trees and 200 strawberry plants. We dug a huge pond that seven ducks and a million frogs immediately adopted as home. I planted wisteria, honeysuckle, and yellow roses. Our garden overflowed with zucchini, tomatoes, and yellow crookneck squash. Our cat had kittens.

I worked with Pinstripe in his business, once again discovering myself to be efficient and full of ideas. Our personal relationship was minimal, but for a while we were both so busy it didn't matter. He thought he had a beautiful, talented wife. The children and I had Oak Crest.

Tension was mounting, but I refused to acknowledge it. Nothing was going to spoil this Red Sea dream-come-true. A heavy silence hung in the air. GirlChild began staying in her room, BoySon in his. Youngest happily followed me around as I prepared supper or did evening chores after work while Pinstripe, settled into a recliner, concentrated on work he brought home. There was order in our home, but it was beginning to stifle us.

It was mostly work and very little play. The only thing we did as a family was go to church. Pinstripe didn't believe we should have a television. Fortunately, my children had come to love books as I did, so they read a lot. But after so many books, boredom set in. Chores were added to dispel restlessness but only aggravated it.

"Why don't we ever do anything?" complained sixteen-year-old GirlChild.

Not allowed to date, she felt especially trapped. I made excuses. I got angry back at her. We scrapped and experienced all the common frustrations of mother and teenage daughter. BoySon withdrew further into his private world. The promise of fathering by Pinstripe shriveled into nothingness. The only thing he did with BoySon was to teach him how to shoot a pistol. I learned, too, and became a good shot.

I held tightly to these times, a piece here and a piece there, the way one might hang onto the pieces of a fractured vase, hoping that everything would hold together. We just needed time.

Pinstripe's dominance became unbearable. He seemed to need to exercise control in order to feel that he was successfully fulfilling his role as a husband. He had definite ideas about a woman's place in life, especially a wife, and therefore his rigidity hit me the hardest. One of his ideas was that a wife belonged in bed with her husband. If I slipped downstairs at night, he came to retrieve me.

At first I gave in, not wanting to upset him. However, one night after an unpleasant discussion I headed downstairs, dug out a sleeping bag, and lay down on a sofa, fully intending to go back upstairs later. I wanted privacy and warmth in which to work through my tears.

In no time Pinstripe came down and demanded that I come back to bed—immediately! I told him I wanted to be alone for a while. When he insisted, I balked. Pinstripe commanded me and I said "No." Without a word, he grabbed my wrists and made me go with him. I was stunned. It was the first time he had used physical force, but it was not to be the last.

At about that time I had purchased a computer for BoySon, hoping to get him interested in something that would fill the empty hours he spent alone in his room. Along with it I bought a small black-and-white TV as a monitor, since it was the cheapest way to go. BoySon quickly improved on the opportunity, secretly using the TV as a source of entertainment. I knew about it, but didn't really care. It seemed a small concession.

One evening Pinstripe asked BoySon if the TV could function as such, to which BoySon said yes. Since Pinstripe wanted to watch something, we all packed into BoySon's bedroom and viewed the program. Another small piece to the vase, I thought hopefully.

With stern admonition that BoySon was not to take our departure from family policy as authorization for general usage, we were allowed to watch TV on those occasions when Pinstripe wanted to. GirlChild rebelled at being told that TV was inherently bad unless there was something on that Pinstripe wanted to watch. Though I agreed with her wholeheartedly, I felt it necessary to back Pinstripe. GirlChild's sarcasm was scalding: Christianity was a joke.

BoySon continued his private exploitation of TV. I warned him that he was begging for trouble, but he didn't care—until the night Pinstripe caught him.

You'd have thought it was Moses on Sinai all over again: righteousness, wrath, and thunder. For a few days, BoySon complied. Then boredom set in again. I told him to stop. I had experienced Pinstripe's forcefulness and did not want it to cross over to the children.

A few nights later Pinstripe caught BoySon at it again. Though BoySon apologized and I promised to take the TV back and purchase a monitor that could not be used as a TV, Pinstripe took it outside and smashed it on the concrete driveway, shouting, "I will not have the devil in our home!"

GirlChild watched the whole process with disgust. In the garage sat a color TV that a customer had given to Pinstripe as payment for services. It needed some repairs, which Pinstripe was planning to make so he could view his programs in color.

"Smash that one too!" she demanded as he performed his righteous act. "If TV is of the devil, then that one is, too!"

Pinstripe ignored her as she stormed upstairs. Soon after that she started sneaking out at night and coming home with liquor on her breath. When Pinstripe caught her, he threatened to turn her in to the police, telling her she'd end up in juvenile court.

"I don't care," she said, her eyes hard. "At least they'll have a TV there!"

Chapter Twenty-six

'Til Death Do Us Part

I picked up the ringing telephone and instantly a cold horror cut through me. Saintman's voice came over the line like a nightmare reborn. GirlChild had evidently contacted him, hoping somehow that she'd been wrong about him—that he was the dad she so longed for.

"I have a right to see my children," he said, his voice low and deliberate. "GirlChild wants to see me."

"If you come near this property, I will call the police," I said.

Though the five years in which he had been legally forbidden to come near us had expired, I knew he would not want to chance another tangle with the law.

"You're not a Christian," he said.

"Takes one to know one," I answered, the fear of him slowly coming under control.

"You've gotten hard," he observed.

"Yup," I said. "Feels great."

"Well, I always knew what kind of woman you were."

It didn't matter what he thought.

"That's right, Saintman. Goodbye," I said, and hung up.

Later I took GirlChild aside and told her that it was her business if she wanted to contact Saintman, but it was not fair to make BoySon face him. She was shocked and dismayed.

"He promised he wouldn't contact you!" she wailed.

I reminded her that Saintman's promises were tools he used indiscriminately to obtain his desired ends.

"Please be careful, GirlChild," I pleaded. "I haven't made up stories about Saintman. They're all true—plus some I never felt it necessary for you to hear."

GirlChild looked miserable. "I'll never call him again."

She did, though. He told her she should leave home, that he'd set her up in an apartment. He sympathized with her complaints and told her I'd kept him from her all these years. GirlChild's rebellion rapidly reached new heights. She began smoking marijuana. Later, she would do crack.

Because of what Saintman told her, GirlChild felt she had an option. She could leave my home any time she wanted. I could see her misery and knew she wanted reasons to stay. She was testing my commitment to her. She needed to know that I would not forsake her. And so we walked a tightrope daily.

One night I awoke at three in the morning and discovered that GirlChild was missing. She had never been gone this late. Pinstripe woke up and suggested we call the police. I agreed, out of fear that something had happened to her. A patrol car was dispatched to our house. While we were waiting its arrival, GirlChild came home.

All my fears exploded. Setting her down on the stairs, I told her I knew what was happening. I had found a letter in which a twenty-two-year-old man apologized for forcing her sexually. I was certain she had been with him and, because I feared for her safety, I had called the police. Pinstripe interrupted me, enraged. He had known nothing of the letter.

"That's statutory rape! He'll go to jail for it!"

GirlChild became extremely agitated, saying she loved the boy and would never testify to such a thing. Pinstripe replied that he was going to press charges anyway. The boy had provided all the evidence anyone would need. His letter was a signed confession!

With a great sob, GirlChild bolted up the stairs and into the bathroom, slamming the door after her. Taking the stairs three at a time, I had just begun talking to her through the door when I heard her pop the top of a medicine bottle off.

Retrieving a key from on top of the molding, I inserted it into the lock and pushed on the door. GirlChild pulled open a cabinet drawer next to it so I couldn't gain entrance. I could see in, however, and spotted an open pill bottle and tablets spilled across the counter. GirlChild was gulping them down.

Screaming, I tried to break through. "Stop! GirlChild! We can work things through!"

Just then the police arrived. Hearing what was going on, they leaped to the top of the stairs and had the door open in seconds. I collapsed onto the floor, crying.

One of the patrolmen took GirlChild aside and questioned her. The other spoke with Pinstripe and me. Then they traded off. We learned that GirlChild had taken only enough tablets to make her sleep through the next day, but her conversation with the officer led him to believe she was too unstable to leave unattended, so they took her to a county mental-health facility where she was committed for no less than three days of observation.

At first GirlChild thought the whole affair was great. It got her out from under our jurisdiction and made her the focus of attention by many people. Then one of the rougher ward members who was somewhat deranged gave her a royal black eye. Suddenly, it was serious business.

She asked her attendants to let her go home, but was given no assurance that she would be released even in three days, nor that she would be sent home when she did leave. There was talk of court custody. Frightened, she called me several times a day, begging me to come and get her, but it was out of my hands. All I could do was love her. I bought her a little stuffed monkey, which she promptly named Monkey Bars since she was, as she put it, behind bars.

After several counseling sessions, GirlChild was released into our custody. She was greatly subdued, but life at home was not.

Pinstripe seemed to have taken a turn for the worse. Ashamed of GirlChild's actions, he felt they reflected on his ability to hold our family in line and blamed it on me for not submitting to him. The fact that we were undergoing financial difficulties seemed to him to confirm his accusations that God obviously was not blessing us. And that it was because I had not learned my place as a woman.

His reasoning distressed me greatly, especially because he continually used religious terms to defend his position. When I said anything, he dismissed my thoughts as ridiculous. Though he was driving me away from him by his coldness, because he was my husband he demanded intimacy as his God-given right. One night I confronted him.

"What right do you have to deal with me so harshly?" I demanded. "It's wrong for you to use your physical strength to force me to 'obey' you. You use God's name, but God is not like that!"

Pinstripe grabbed my wrists, squeezed them tightly, and said, "Of course He is. Haven't you read the Old Testament?"

He was hurting me. "Let go!" I demanded. "Your maleness is no excuse for you to demand that I comply to your wishes. My feelings count too!"

"Your feelings are out of line!" he shot back. "When will you learn your place as a woman?"

"It's not a woman's place to submit to a man's cruelty," I began.

Suddenly the strength went out of me. Too much had been happening. I fell to my knees, exhausted, my head coming to rest against his legs.

"That's better," he said, releasing my wrists. "Why don't you submit like this more often?"

I was crying. "I hate you," I said softly.

And I did. I never hated W.H. or Guy—or even Saintman, whom I feared greatly. Fear I could accept in myself. But now I hated Pinstripe, and Christians aren't supposed to hate. It was like admitting that now I *was* the bad one. I had reached a new low. Shame engulfed me, and it made me hate him even more for making me feel that way.

Pinstripe stood there inflicting hurt yet feeling no guilt, while I was smitten with the knowledge that I hated. Bowed before him, I fought with all my heart to hold onto what I was learning about God. It would take me many months to work through these feelings.

It wasn't long before GirlChild called Saintman again. She asked him to rent the apartment he'd promised her. He told her that she should get emancipated, meaning declared legally of age. She really liked that idea and sought out an attorney friend to take care of this for her.

The attorney called Saintman to see what was really going on and asked him if he planned on covering the fee for this service. Saintman claimed he never promised GirlChild financial help, but said he felt that she should be emancipated.

As they talked, the attorney quickly discovered that Saintman had no real interest in GirlChild's welfare. He was striking back at me. He told GirlChild that he felt Saintman was not a good man and that she should be careful of him.

"Your mother loves you," he admonished. "Trust her."

"I know she does," GirlChild replied. "She's the only one who ever has."

This encounter crushed GirlChild badly. She seemed more lost than ever, and our deteriorating family life didn't help matters. All she wanted to do was to get away and I couldn't blame her. She was tired of turmoil, tired of religious words being wrapped around hatefulness. So was I, but I had determined to stick it out—till death do us part.

Several months later, GirlChild received a call from a district attorney in a city several hours away. Saintman asked that she be called as a character witness; he'd been arrested for murder. GirlChild cried, telling the man that if she testified they'd lock Saintman up for life.

"Oh, Mommy! It could have been you!" she cried. She hadn't let me touch her for a long time, but now I held her in my arms, rocking her. Suddenly she pulled back, her eyes wide with fear.

"It could have been *me*! I'm so glad I never went to see him! Oh, Mommy!"

Saintman is now serving a life sentence in a state penitentiary for the murder of his eighteen-year old girlfriend. GirlChild herself was only seventeen.

Not long after that I learned I was pregnant. Pinstripe was euphoric, but also keenly aware that our marriage was in deep trouble. He sat me down and told me that if we separated, I had my three children. This child was his and I'd better get that straight right from the start. It made me remember something he'd said early in our marriage during one of the rare occasions we spent time alone.

We had gone to a small cafe up in the mountains—a truck stop, really. There were kerosene lanterns on oil-clothed tables. We ordered cornbread and hot chocolate. The pungent smell of kerosene mixed with oldness gave the place an unobtrusive, romantic feeling. My heart ached for warmth and love. Pinstripe leaned across the table toward me, looking for a long moment into my eyes. I thought he was going to speak intimately.

Instead he said, "I will not stay married to a woman who does not obey me."

Though I did not want to have a baby, how could I agree to what Pinstripe said? I could never give up one of my children! Fortunately, I never had to find out because in my fourth month my body gave up the child. On the way home from the hospital, Pinstripe told me that I hadn't been worth marrying. If I couldn't bear him a son, our marriage was in vain.

Even though I did not want a child by Pinstripe, the loss of this baby broke my heart. Every child I carried I had loved long before it was born. This one was no different. As I looked out the car window I saw the sky arching above the hills, blue and clean. Never in my life had I felt so estranged from this world. Longings that no human language can ever express filled my heart. I wanted to go *Home*; I wanted to be with the Father.

Later, alone at last, I poured out my heart to God.

Father, it is too much. Am I being punished for my sins? Somehow, I cannot believe this is true. You continue to draw me to yourself. No matter what, I cannot quit now. I've come too far. The only thing I have left to ask is that you save my children. If you know they would be better off with someone else, please let me die. Guy has remarried. He seems to love Youngest. Do you want her to go with him?

Youngest's face rose before me. I remembered how she cried and clung to me whenever Guy came to get her. He had to peel her away from me. She needed me, at least for a while. Or did she? I didn't know what to do. Three failed marriages, and now a fourth. Every decision I'd ever made seemed to rise before me as failure.

Oh, Father! How can I know these things? You seem to hide from me when I pray. After all the grief I've brought to my little family, do you really want me to keep making my own decisions? Why don't you just let me die? I'll never bring you honor now!

I was in the process of declaring myself totally unacceptable. To myself and everyone else. How could I ever hope to rise above all my failures? My poor children!

Please, Father, I'm not good for anything. I give you my children. Just let me come Home!

As I spoke, my agitation left me and, though I looked for it, I could not find it. I had landed on my Eagle-Father's back.

Chapter Twenty-seven

Her Father's Child

I knew it was wrong to hate. What I didn't understand was the process whereby God heals the human spirit. Were He to magically remove my hatred for Pinstripe, He would have to amputate an important part of my emotions. Instead He worked to redirect these negative energies so I could be free at last from the deficiency of my upbringing.

When emotional pain cuts deeply into the heart, many Christians accept the injury but think the "scabbing" process is sin. In reality it's just as much nature's way of healing, as are physical scabs that prevent germs from infecting a bodily wound.

Anger sometimes develops as a natural, temporary covering for a soul that has sustained emotional gashes. Anger can fester into hatred, spreading despair like bacteria throughout the system. In bodily injury, if unattended, this may cause death.

I came to realize that my anger toward Pinstripe was like a scab. It was a natural response to years of injustice and pain. But God wanted me to see my hatred as a warning—as a festering infection that could cost me eternal life if I failed to deal with it. He was alerting me to the fact that I needed to overcome the feelings of inferiority that infected my whole being.

Though at first all I could see was Pinstripe, I slowly became aware that *I* was the real enemy. I viewed myself as a victim and therefore remained one. Granted, I had entered this world disadvantaged by my parents' deeply troubled lifestyle, but I did not have to let this keep on deciding my destiny.

My thoughts turned again to the process of ceramic making. I had hoped for so much! Was I living proof that God's promises can be as useless as broken pottery? I knew that I had not forsaken Him, but where had I gone wrong?

I went to the woods to confront myself. I took personal inventory as I walked along, and made a startling discovery. Very candidly, for the first time in my life, I realized that, except for my poor choices in marriage partners, I liked the person I was becoming. For several years the people I worked for had told me that I was industrious and thorough. They complimented me on my ability to leave an entire office in much better shape than I found it. I thrived on challenges, and people trusted me and sought my advice.

"I *do* have something useful to offer the world!" I thought. "My life is *not* a failure." Excitement for life and love for people filled my heart. I realized that I was still my Father's child! But if that was true, what about the hatred I felt? Surely, God's children know no hatred.

When I talked to Shepherd, he told me that my hatred did not mean I had cut myself off from the Father. To me, it seemed like a contradiction. How could one be united to God, who is Love, and experience hatred? I began to examine how I felt when I hated Pinstripe.

Immediately it came to me that I associated Pinstripe with bondage to my low self-esteem. In order to "obey" him and accept his concept of a woman's place in life I had to forfeit both my hard won sense of personal worth and my understanding of God.

Everything in me rose up against this! It was as if my very soul was in an act of expulsion. It was not conceit that made me see myself as deserving of respect. In rejecting the demons of self-destruction and worthlessness, I was fighting for God's honor as well as my own!

I realized that it was not Pinstripe I hated, but everything he

stood for. In resisting him, I was repudiating my own poorer self.
No wonder God did not want to amputate my wrong feelings!
Rather, He and I worked together to set me free. He allowed
me to retain the energy by which I would forever shake off the
shackles of my past. It was up to me to consciously harness my
emotions in order to make them my servants rather than my
taskmasters.

I was still pondering the metaphor of ceramics when I got
back to the house. On an impulse, I called a local ceramics shop.
I asked the woman who answered if ceramic dishes ever needed
to be fired again after the colors had been set.

"Yes, of course," she replied. "That's what makes them safe to
eat off of." She went on to explain the dangers of lead poison-
ing.

"Safe to eat off of?" I repeated wondrously. "Thank you!
Thank you so much!"

Replacing the phone on its cradle, I knelt down.

*Father—safe to eat off of! Are you making me safe to eat off of?
Does that mean that you are going to serve yourself to others through
me? I want this more than anything in life. First, for my children,
and then for anyone of your choosing who is hungry for you. How
hungry for you I have been all my life! Surely, if you can do this for
and through me, there is hope for anyone. Anyone!*

Later that evening BoySon, who attended boarding school,
came home for the weekend. Though I felt it was a good thing
for him to live away from the turmoil in our home, I increasingly worried about him. He was withdrawn. He said he felt
stupid around other kids because he never knew what to say.
I knew he needed to overcome this growing introversion or it
might be bottled inside of him for life.

After he had settled into his room, I went in to talk to him.
He was lying on his bed, staring at the ceiling. I lay down next to
him and asked him how things were going. At first he didn't answer me. Finally he mumbled some words I could barely hear.

"BoySon," I began, "I'm going to help you talk. I know it's
easier to withdraw into silence, but I'm not going to let you do

that. I know you really don't want to, either. I'm here to listen. Just start talking—about anything. It doesn't matter what."

For a time he said nothing, then began telling me about an incident that happened at school. He spoke haltingly, became angry and clammed up. I prodded and coaxed until he said more. I asked questions to draw him out. It was grueling. Both of us were worn out after a half hour.

From then on it became a ritual. Whenever he came home, that was the night I went in for a debriefing. Sometimes he turned on me, letting his frustration and fury fall on my head. At those times I lay very still, letting hot tears slip down the side of my face. It took all the control I could muster. I verbally agreed with him. He had every right to his feelings.

Slowly, BoySon began to express himself more easily. He even chatted a little. We laughed together, and he wanted to know how I felt about things. We talked a lot about God. We became friends. We were out of the woods.

Pinstripe and I were entering the darkest of forests. Though I was getting a handle on my hatred, I could not make myself like him. He was so arbitrary and unfeeling. He told me that he wished I'd leave him, but first I owed him a child. After I gave him a child, I could just get out. I could even get out sooner, as long as I agreed to bear him an heir.

His words stung and insulted me. I told him that he was the littlest man I had ever known. To think that a woman could be ordered to produce a child, as if she were some sort of factory, was totally beyond my comprehension.

I could not stand for Pinstripe to touch me. He obviously did not love me; why should he use me? We argued a lot over this. He told me that when I married him I had given up my rights over my body.

I could not believe my ears! Sometimes, when our arguing became intense, he pushed me down and sat on my chest, pinning my hands down in a surrender position. The first few times I just cried and begged for him to come to his senses. Then I started fighting back with every ounce of strength I had and tried to bite his hands. Like a cornered animal, I would rather have died in my own blood than be taken captive. At those moments I wasn't so sure it was just my past that I hated.

Though he continually told me to leave him, I did not. The thought of another broken marriage was unthinkable to me. He began to threaten suicide. I still worked in his business. Several times he sat on the windowsill of his office, eight stories up, shouting at me that he was going to throw himself to his death. I pled with him to get back inside, but this only made him worse. Finally I would leave the office, figuring if I was not there to watch, he'd lose the incentive. Whenever I came back, he was always at his desk.

Once he came home from target practice, his gun strapped to his belt. He paced the room, talking about how he couldn't take it anymore. At one point, he came close to me and said very quietly, "I hope I never hurt you." After he calmed down I asked him what he meant, but he denied ever saying such a thing. I was becoming frightened. He started keeping his gun under his pillow. Loaded.

One day he called me from the office and told me that he couldn't stand it any longer. He was heading for a bridge about a mile from his office. Then he hung up. Two hours later he called back, never mentioning the previous conversation.

I went upstairs, removed his gun from under his pillow, and hid it. If any of us was going to die, it would not be by that gun! When he found it missing that night, he was furious and demanded I give it back to him immediately. I told him I had hidden it for his own safety as well as for the rest of us. He said I was being ridiculous, but I still would not tell him where it was hidden. He dropped the subject.

Though I continually prayed for guidance, I knew by now that God was not going to write any answers in the sky. He wanted to write His character into my heart. This time it was all or nothing. The eaglet had landed on its Father's back and was being carried upward for another try at flight.

Christmas came. My heart sparkled with every tiny light on

every green tree. When the snow fell, I ran out to greet it, glad for my Father's promise of "whiter than snow." My spirit was dancing and there was hope in the nativity songs in the night. The New Year was upon us, and I was stretching toward newness of life.

It happened the night before New Year's Eve. Pinstripe and I were lying far apart on our king-sized waterbed. I no longer remember what started it, only that he began to shove me out of bed with his feet. Then he was sitting on my chest, yelling at me.

He put his hands on my neck and began to squeeze. I screamed for help, but he only squeezed harder. The room began to spin, and I seemed almost out of my body. I heard my own voice, faint and eerie, high above the scene. I knew I was going to die.

The bedroom door flew open, and GirlChild's voice broke through my consciousness. "What is the meaning of this?" she demanded.

Pinstripe let go of my neck, and I rolled toward the edge of the bed and onto the floor. "Everything is under control," he said. "Go back to bed."

GirlChild, not realizing the severity of the situation, left the room.

"No! Don't leave me!" I called after her.

I had not regained my full senses yet, or I would have told her and BoySon to run away as fast as they could. Pinstripe seemed confused and wanted everything quiet and back to normal. I stumbled out of the bedroom and headed for BoySon's room, Pinstripe at my heels.

BoySon, his hair tousled, rose on one elbow and asked what was going on. I crawled onto BoySon's bed and lay down beside him, shaking uncontrollably.

"He was strangling me. Please don't let him take me," I begged.

Pinstripe took hold of one of my arms. "Come on. Don't make a big deal out of it. Let's go back to bed."

BoySon, in a slow, deliberate movement, put his right arm across my body.

"She's staying here," he said firmly, in a voice sounding much older than his fifteen years.

"Don't interfere, BoySon." Pinstripe sounded irritated, but subdued.

BoySon's voice was steady. "When she wants to go, she can go, but she's not going until she's ready."

They argued over my head for a little while. I was so tired; I wanted to go to sleep. My mind seemed to want to put the incident to rest.

Somehow we got to morning, the last day of the old year. I called a close friend and told her what had happened. She was adamant: "Get out of there!"

I told her that I just couldn't, that I'd been married four times.

"Yeah? Well, you can only die once!" she snapped.

Chapter Twenty-eight

The Frog

New Year's Day came and went. Birds chirped their announcement of the morning, and stars pinned up the night. The next day I noticed the laundry was building up again. Youngest had left a dolly outside by the pond. It looked like a little leprechaun scouting out frogland. I was very tired, and everything seemed a little disconnected. Why did life just go on as if nothing traumatic had happened? Was this the edge of insanity?

My friend called back with a message from a well-known minister: Leave as quickly as possible! Instead, I found a marriage counselor and persuaded Pinstripe to go with me.

The story Pinstripe told was so different from mine! He said he'd only been shaking my shoulders, not even touching my throat. Later, he denied even that. Then he quit going, saying he had received all the help he needed, but I certainly needed to keep going. I went, hungry to find hope for our marriage, even though it felt like I was trying to comb the burrs out of a lion's mane with a matchstick.

GirlChild was getting completely out of hand. She seemed to want to test me—and God— to the limit. Though we fought over everything, I told her that nothing would ever make me stop loving her. I would be there as long as I lived. She could count on it. I think she believed the same about God, because she genuinely believed me. It was a small but cherished victory.

The months slipped by. When GirlChild neared eighteen she

decided to move in with a girlfriend and her grandparents. The day she left I cried for hours. I loved her so much, but I couldn't spare her the agony of where she was headed. Also, it seemed only a matter of time until our home disintegrated. Better that GirlChild not be around to blame herself when it happened.

As it turned out, it was just a little over two months later that Pinstripe told me I had one week to get out. I decided it was time to go. The summer was coming and BoySon was due home. Since the New Year's incident he didn't want to live at home anymore. I didn't blame him. That weekend friends helped me move to a tiny place in the hills. As I said my goodbyes to Oak Crest, I didn't ever want to hold a dream to my heart again.

That summer the children and I grew tan and happy. I hid from the world and it didn't miss me. We spent a lot of time with Shepherd and his family. Shepherd's wife was great fun. We enjoyed each other's company and I was comforted by her steadfast loyalty. Any comments that came her way concerning me were met with staunch rebuttals. It was just what the doctor ordered. It gave me back some skin.

Our home in the hills was near a grove of trees, and among these trees I found a little retreat. There were ferns in my quiet chapel and I could hear the sound of water running through the undergrowth, seemingly unperplexed and joyous. A million tiny things grew everywhere like a secret kingdom that someone forgot to spoil.

I found happiness in the simple stirrings of nature: the wind that scooted between the branches of the live oaks, rattling leaves like paper chimes, the sound of woodland creatures unaware of my presence. I never wanted to go back to dwell among paved streets and cemented hearts again.

One afternoon, as I was sorting through some of my things, I came across my mother's old Bible from her childhood days. She had given it to me when cleaning out her trunk. The binding was worn and the pages yellowed. It was over sixty years old.

Mom.

My mother and brother still lived together. He never left

home, never got a job, never discovered normal life. There were times when he didn't leave their apartment for a year at a time. At forty, he still loved teddy bears. Between the two of them they owned sixteen of them. When I visited, he usually retrieved one of them and peeked it around the corner at me, his face boyish and untried. I found this devastating. He had never made it out of the pit.

As my mind searched for reasons, that vivid, lurid picture of my father sitting on my mother's chest as he strangled her came forcefully to mind. But this time the memory oscillated between striped bib overalls and a pinstriped suit. In my imagination I stood on the stairs and watched, yet felt "his" hands around my neck—whose hands were they? Either way, the scream was mine.

Shaken, I realized my life had come full circle. What I did, where I went, and who I became was totally up to me now. If only I could be rid of the awful stigma of so many failed marriages! Pinstripe told me it was senseless to keep a paper alliance, so we filed jointly for divorce. It was very hard for me to accept.

I put Mom's Bible away and knelt by the couch.

Father, help me to put away these memories. Help me to start over again. I feel so ugly. If only things had been different. I know that in your eyes I am a favored child, but the rest of the world isn't going to see it that way.

A few weeks later I received a phone call from a young woman who asked me to share my faith with a group of teenage girls. I was shocked! *Me*, the all-time loser? But, remembering the hunger of my own youth, I accepted. Had not God promised to make me a safe plate upon which He could serve Himself to others? And so passed a fruitful weekend. A tiny sprig of hope began to grow in my heart.

Shortly after that this same young woman asked if I might be interested in sharing my faith with other groups as well. Though the thought of it frightened me, I did not decline immediately, but promised to have lunch with her and her mother to discuss it further. I took Youngest along to make a day of it afterward at a park.

As we ate our lunch, the young woman's mother, herself a divorcee who had remarried several years before, was cordial but reserved. The more we talked, the more uncomfortable I became. Finally I said that I would have to be awfully sure that everyone was comfortable with the fact that I had been married several times. The mother turned to me and asked with visible control, "How many times *have* you been married?"

I wanted to run, because I knew what was coming. My unacceptability loomed before me. Why had I agreed to this meeting anyway? I should have known better. I had only added stupidity to my undesirableness. A horrible lump fixed itself in my throat. I felt sick to my stomach.

"Four times," I replied, my eyes stinging.

Though I wanted desperately to explain, no words left my mouth. Mentally, I saw her count on her fingers: one, two, three, four. She drew in a breath.

"Well, you have certainly disqualified yourself. You could only speak to a very selected group of people."

"Yes," I thought to myself, "sinners—the scabby kind, not the decent, church-going type. People who need the Father as badly as I do." I said some nice words to the ladies to make them feel they had not offended me or cut through to the center of my soul. I said the words and fled with my little girl to a park where a train ran through the trees.

The lump in my throat ached as we rode, but I could not cry. I could not trouble Youngest with my sorrow. After a time, we climbed back into our car and headed home. Youngest was soon fast asleep, smudged and happy with the day's activities. A low groan began deep inside me. Tears washed down my cheeks, hot and unchecked.

Oh Father, I feel like I've discovered I have cancer, only cancer victims get to die. I have to keep living with horrible holes eaten out of my spirit. The stench of my malady is a reproach to others. How else could it be? How else could they feel?

To my mind came a picture of a room full of dancers in their splendid garments. I watched them whirl about the floor.

Father, I can dance too! I know that my garments don't bear the proper labels, and I did not learn my steps in an appropriate way, yet my heart is full of your music. My energy seems to have no limit, but I am being pushed from the floor and told that the very things that taught me how to dance have disqualified me. Oh Father, let me dance. Please, let me dance!

My heart was so full of God I felt as though it would explode. At the same time I felt shut up, away from the place of celebration. This new sorrow continued to cloud my world for many weeks. When I mingled with others, I felt I was somehow being dishonest. If they knew the truth about my life, they probably would not choose to have me in their midst. I felt unworthy to accept their friendship. It was mine by default of their courtesy. They must have four fingers hidden somewhere: one, two, three, four.

I wanted them to know; yet I was terrified they might find out. If only I could stay in the hills forever! But the hills could never satisfy me. Having come to know the Father, I had fallen in love with the human race. Night after night this sorrow bore down upon my heart. If only there was something I could do!

And then came the frog.

I heard him somewhere in our front room. Though I searched for him diligently, I could not find him. All during the night he croaked, making sleep difficult. In the morning I still couldn't find him. The days passed, the frog happily hidden somewhere out of my careful scrutiny while the house began to smell like a pond. I had to get rid of that frog!

Finally I spotted him on my piano, next to the little carved animals that were Youngest's. He was partially hidden by an ivy plant. I picked him up and placed him out on the back deck.

A couple of nights later I heard him again. How in the world had he gotten back in? We searched high and low but could not find him. His odor hung in the air. A few days later I caught him again—on the piano. Not a little distressed, this time I threw him from the patio some eight feet down. I felt a faint twinge of guilt. He probably landed okay, I told myself. At least he won't be back.

A week later a familiar croaking filled our home again. I wondered if it was a family of frogs. On an impulse, I looked toward the piano. Sure enough, there he sat. I was getting desperate. Youngest watched me as I grabbed him and headed for the bathroom.

"What are you going to do, Mommy?" she asked.

I made her stay in the front room. Lifting the lid, I pulled the toilet handle and threw in the frog. Legs splayed, he rode the spiraling water momentarily then disappeared with a glug.

Youngest, who was not yet six years old, did not understand what happens when you flush a toilet.

"Is he outside in the field?" she queried.

"Sort of," I answered.

"A drain field," I thought to myself ruefully.

That night I returned to the bathroom and nearly fainted. There sat the frog on the edge of the bowl, looking slightly drugged but quite alive. I lost my senses. It was a battle now. I had to get rid of that frog! Snatching him up, I ran outside to the edge of a bank some hundred feet from the house. I hurled the frog with all my might. Off he sailed into the darkness. I felt like a murderer.

Several days went by. The frog did not reappear, and I had all but forgotten him. It was nighttime again, and I was lying in bed, talking to God about the grief I felt over my past. I just didn't know what to do.

"Crooo—aaak. Crooo—aaak," came the familiar call of the frog and, with it, a suspicion that this was no usual occurrence.

Slipping out of bed, I reached for a flashlight and headed for the front room. If it was the same frog, I knew exactly where he'd be. Holding my breath, I aimed a yellow beam at the piano. There, just under the ivy plant, sat the frog.

"Oh, no!" I whispered to myself. My remorse had caught up with me, and I could do him no further harm. Getting an empty margarine container, I punched holes in the lid and imprisoned the frog inside.

"There!" I said. "You've been through enough. I'll decide what to do with you in the morning. I apologize for being so awful to you."

I returned to bed, my mind racing. I suspected God was using this little frog to get my attention. I could no more rid myself of my past than I could remove this smelly little creature from my home. The more I tried, the more I ended up doing regrettable things that didn't work.

So, Father, what do I do?

"Give him to me. I'll take care of everything."

The next morning Youngest and I dressed and readied ourselves for church. When we arrived, I walked to a nearby field and released my little friend.

He's all yours, Father.

Raising my eyes to the clean blue canopy overhead, I nodded.

My past too!

Smiling, I walked back to the church and joined in the worship of the God I trusted with all my heart. I don't know where the frog is today. Probably dead by now. I never saw him again.

Chapter Twenty-nine

This Is Only the Beginning

Spring is a time for new beginnings. I witnessed tender green shoots pushing their way up through the soil and knew that my time in the woods must soon come to an end. It had been a retreat, a gentle place where nature ministered to my bruised spirit. We were friends, solitude and I. Our parting would never be absolute.

Much had happened during my year of seclusion. Most difficult was that GirlChild took a terrible plunge into self-destruction. After graduation she moved in with a young man who leached her of every resource she had. Heavily into drugs, she also became anorexic and landed in the hospital.

At one point, she lived in slum housing where murder and rape were the norm. So I "kidnapped" her. I called her one-day and told her I was sending a friend to pick her up. She would stay with this friend for two weeks; then she would be taken several hundred miles away to live with a family who would help her to rehabilitate.

Of course, GirlChild said she would not go.

"Be ready in two hours," I said.

"Never!" she replied firmly.

When my friend arrived, GirlChild readily went with her, complaining all the time that she was being kidnapped. My friend just chuckled and stopped to get her a milkshake and fries. Later, GirlChild bragged about my love for her. Her life was out of control. It must have felt good to have someone love her enough to step in and do for her what she didn't have the strength to do for herself.

It was hard at first, but she quit drugs, got a job, and started taking some class work. Eventually, she graduated from nursing school with top grades. We became the best of friends. I am a happy grandmother to two of her children.

I moved away from my beloved hills, got a job, and began to once again flourish with responsibility and challenge. Each semester I take a class at a nearby college. I have written several articles that have been published and co-authored a book that has wide distribution. Occasionally I accept speaking appointments.

For the most part, though, I am mother to Youngest, who is now in school. BoySon entered college and is doing very well scholastically. He is well adjusted and friendly. I am proud of him. Only when I help my last eaglet into the sky will I have time to catch my breath.

Not long after I resettled, a concerned friend called to inform me that Pinstripe was claiming "Bible grounds" and remarrying. It upset her to think that people would automatically assume the worst about me. There was no way I was going to get back into the mud pen!

"Forget it," I told her.

If fighting Pinstripe all over again was the only way to validate myself, I'd have to pass. God had given me a promise. I would let Him keep it.

On an impulse, though, two days before the wedding was to take place I called Pinstripe.

"Hello," I said when he answered the phone. "I understand congratulations are in order."

There was a long pause.

"That's right," he said haltingly.

"Pinstripe," I continued, "some of my friends are concerned because you are claiming 'Bible grounds' as your basis for remarriage. Now, don't be alarmed. I have no intention of causing any problems. But just out of curiosity, could you tell me what they are?"

There was another long pause, after which Pinstripe admitted that his Bible grounds were not "the conventional kind," although he assured me he had worked this through with God. Our marriage had been "inappropriate," and thus he was free to remarry. I wished him well, many children, and hung up. It was a warm day and there were no clouds in the sky.

I love to walk along the ocean, and go there whenever I can. Sometimes it is the only thing that will settle the world back down to livable terms. When I hear the enormity of voice that is the ocean's I am reminded of my Father, whose voice called forth our very existence.

Allowing the water-thunder to vibrate through my body, I remember with my whole being that a person's life on this planet is only transitory. My sorry trek has, in fact, only fleeting significance in the greater panorama of eternity. I will not count my two score and four earthly years as wasted, because through them I have come to know the living God. I have walked with bleeding calluses, but I have also soared on eagle's wings.

I'll never forget when it occurred to me that my life was probably not even half over. There is so much living yet to do—so much to learn, so many things to be experienced! I would not be honest if I did not admit that there are times when I still cry in the night, but I have chosen to take my "readings" in the brightness of the day.

I keep a small ceramic frog on my piano, near an ivy plant. God is still taking care of things. I have learned to love reality, even though that reality undeniably includes the fact that I have been where nobody else would ever want to go. I never forget, however, that it was there that I was taken into the very presence of the Almighty!

My Father's breath is warm. By this I mean that He is not an insulted Deity living on the other side of the universe. He does not tolerate us because Jesus begs Him to. He sent Jesus so we could learn to tolerate *Him*, and perhaps even come to love Him as He so loves us. It took many years for these realities to replace those tragic concepts supplied to me by men who, by birth or by ceremony, stood in authority over me.

The Hebrew word for authority denotes strength. In the Greek there is an implication of privilege. I have come to believe that our great God, whose authority is matchless and beyond human expression, is so courteous that He considers it a privilege to exercise His strength on our behalf. He loves to give us ample reason to trust that He has our best interest in His heart. Our Father is an exquisite Gentleman!

Samuel put it this way: "When one rules over men in righteousness, when he rules in the fear of God, he is like the light of morning at sunrise on a cloudless morning, like the brightness after rain that brings the grass from the earth" (2 Samuel 23:3, 4, NIV).

Grass is tender. So must we treat human hearts.

It is our Father's purpose to give us hope.

"'I know the plans I have for you,' declares the Lord, 'plans to prosper you and not to harm you, plans to give you hope and a future'" (Jeremiah 29:11, NIV).

God knows all too well that "hope deferred makes the heart sick, but a longing fulfilled is a tree of life" (Proverbs 13:12, NIV).

For many years I was heartsick almost beyond human endurance, but I have found in God the deepest satisfaction for every longing in my soul.

My Father has hidden the treasure of the knowledge of Himself in me, only a clay jar of ill repute, to show His all-surpassing power to redeem to the uttermost. Because of this, though I have been hard pressed on every side, I have not been crushed. I am still sometimes perplexed, but not in despair. I may be persecuted, but He will never abandon me. If I am struck down, I shall not be destroyed (see 2 Corinthians 4:7-9, NIV).

Oh, My Father, You heard the desire of one of your afflicted. You encouraged me and listened to my cry. You defended me because, in the most real sense, I was fatherless and oppressed. Consequently, man, who is of the earth, can terrify me no more (see Psalm 10:17, 18).

You let me dance! You removed my sackcloth and clothed me with joy. My heart sings to you and cannot be silent. Father, I will give you thanks forever! (see Psalm 30:11, 12)

For me, this is only the beginning—the beginning of joy!

A Letter from Shepherd

Dear EsthersChild:

I have been reflecting on that occasion some thirteen years ago when I first met you, and upon the privilege that has been mine to have a front-row seat in the pilgrimage of your life. It is a reflection that moves me profoundly.

I recall my amazement as the script of your early life began to unfold. As the broken pieces of those years became evident to me, I could only feel great wonder at the energy and vision you brought to your quest for something better. And then I began to discover why.

Though you often engaged in brisk and warm conversation about health, literature, the church and theology, the subtleties of human relationships, and even music (some of which you composed!), there was always one theme that dominated your conscious horizon: You wanted to understand and vitally interact with your heavenly Father! And that quest has been so marked with delight, so rooted in blunt self-honesty, so punctuated with laughter and wit, and so grounded in Scripture, that—perhaps more than you will ever know— you drew many of us into that same quest with you.'

More than ink on paper can ever tell, I stand in your debt. You are the only one I have ever known who consistently and directly challenged me to reach to my highest, to soar to the lofty places, to not discredit our Father by mediocrity. Though

I am myself an ordained minister, I have found in your spiritual quest a tangible attractiveness, a compelling relevance that has drawn me through the dark hours in my own journey. In your presence, speaking the things of God is so natural, so vitalizing, so balanced, so integrated with real life, that it has become the most spontaneous and enjoyable topic between us.

You are a life-toucher, an enabler of good things in others. You will recall that recently several of us planned a birthday party for you. As the party commenced, I sat in a comer and watched the guests arrive to call you blessed. Besides the usual "happy birthdays," with laughter and with tears, they looked to you as a critical turning point in their lives.

Though I have seen you bear the most crushing loads of pain, I have also seen you struggle to the top—in order that you might lift another's load. You make the servant ministry of Jesus authentic in the flesh. Someday, when our Lord gives us each wings, my first lessons in soaring will have been learned, and in His name, I will thank you again.

To His glory, Shepherd

Epilogue

When I began to write this manuscript, it was specifically for my children and was meant to help them make some sense out of the tangled threads of their lives. I didn't get very far. It made me so sick I had to burn it in the fireplace to get well.

A year later, I started again. I had achieved some success co-authoring a daily devotional book, and a publishing house called to ask me if I was working on another manuscript. I told them I was not. They argued with me, saying that they had heard that I was writing a book.

"It is not for publication," I informed them. They continued to call me about it even though I told them it was not something anyone else would want to read. It was for my children. "What if it helps someone?" they responded. How could I refuse? I was deeply conscious of all the years I needed help. The rest is history.

To my surprise, under its original title, *Light Through the Dark Glass*, my book won an Angel Award in 1990. Even though it was the publisher's first award of this kind for a book, they chose to let it go out of print a year later to avoid growing controversy. It was not an easy read for their traditional customers.

I have grown a great deal in the nineteen years since I first wrote this book, and my view of life has broadened considerably. My reference points have changed dramatically. I no longer am defined by the very intense, religious context in which this story transpired.

Abuse recovery is by its very nature an often unsuccessful endeavor. And, when it is successful, what often happens is that exchanges are made instead of going the distance to true liberation. Like a smoker who substitutes food for cigarettes and then must battle obesity rather than the possibility of lung cancer, people can settle into the first stages of success and end up being stuck. Though surely a better place, they are still not in a truly healthy state. To some, my story is a testimony of the power of God in a damaged life, which it is. But to stop there would be like thinking childhood is the best life has to offer.

EsthersChild has grown into an adult woman who still marvels at the exquisite beauty of nature, but finds equal pleasure just reading a book or talking to a friend about everyday life. In fact, my life has become very ordinary and pleasantly common. Those who know me now would not guess that such a story could be mine.

So why am I resurrecting my book? Exactly for this reason. Because those who are still captives of abuse, or who are in recovery, can understand they do not need to continue to relive their pain or carry their story consciously with them forever. Though intrinsically a part of them, they are free to unbuckle their seatbelts and move about life uninhibited.

As I make this manuscript about transcending the negative, dominant scripting of childhood available to a wider readership, I know it is for women who are rising like a phoenix from the ashes of their dreams. However, personal tragedy is not a prerequisite for finding its pages poignant to the struggles all women face.

In 2004 a friend of mine, the director of a women's shelter, asked me if I could find a prayer or poem that could be used at their recovery meetings. When I wasn't able to find anything I felt suitable, I offered to write one. I wrote *Merit Born*, which was subsequently translated into Spanish.

I pictured battered women standing together, arms dropped

to their sides, waiting. How many years I waited for relief and healing! How often I could have used a mantra to repeat to myself as I struggled against the currents of a damaged self-image.

I have learned that I was born with as much merit as anyone.

I know I deserve to be treated with respect and equality.

I accept only a crown of light, for I am beautiful, and strong, and free.

GirlChild, who became an R.N., has gone through substance abuse recovery. She still struggles with her life, but is working through her pain successfully. Her two teenage children are intelligent and insightful members of our growing little family.

BoySon graduated from law school in the top two percent of his class with the Order of Coif. He is an attorney in an established law firm in Northern California. Married to a lovely woman, they have three delightful, young children.

Youngest is married to a career firefighter, and enjoys her job as Project Manager in an architecture firm.

And me? I have commuted my "sentence" of being a victim of abuse.

My Darkness has been Overturned!

Merit Born

I am Woman— Sister, Spouse
Equal Master of my House
Inside, Outside, Merit Born
Crown of Glory not of Thorns
Daughters Equal to our Sons
Worthy, Rightful, Splendid Ones
Free and Able, Gold not Dirt
I have Risen from my Hurt
Soaring Higher every Day
Equal Being, Equal Pay
Joining hands We Claim our Place
Sing our Songs by Heaven's Grace

—*EsthersChild*, March 2004

Mérito Nacido

Yo soy mujer, hermanaa, esposa,
Ama igual de mi hogar
Adentro, afuera, mérito nacido,
Corona de gloria, no de espinas
Hijas iguales que nuestros hijos,
Valiosas, derechas, espléndidas
Libres y capaces; oro, no barro,
He Salido de mi dolor
Elevándrome cada día más alto,
Ser igual, igual paga
Tomadas de manos,
Reclamamos nuestro lugar
Canta nuestros cantos,
Por la gracia del cieto.

—*EsthersChild*, 2004

CPSIA information can be obtained at www.ICGtesting.com
Printed in the USA
BVOW08s2252121115

426915BV00001B/6/P